Ragon

# MILITARY UNIFORMS, 1686-1918

# A GROSSET ALL-COLOR GUIDE

# MILITARY UNIFORMS, 1686-1918

## BY RENE NORTH

## Illustrated by John Berry

Supervising Editor ....... Georg Zappler

*Board of Consultants*

Richard G. Van Gelder ....... Chairman and Curator, Mammals, American Museum of Natural History

William C. Steere .......... Director, New York Botanical Gardens

Sune Engelbrektson ......... Space Science Co-ordinator, Port Chester Public Schools

John F. Middleton .......... Chairman, Anthropology, New York University

Carl M. Kortepeter .......... Associate Professor, History, New York University

Michael Cohn ............. Curator, Cultural History, Brooklyn Children's Museum

Frank X. Critchlow ......... Consulting Engineer, Applied and Theoretical Electronics

## GROSSET & DUNLAP
### A NATIONAL GENERAL COMPANY
Publishers • New York

# FOREWORD

To attempt a condensed history of military dress in a small volume may seem reckless in the extreme, and this book cannot possibly claim to be a complete survey of the subject. However, by presenting the study under the headings of campaigns rather than countries, a new and more interesting approach is achieved.

Even so, there must of necessity be some gaps. Also, many instances occur where authorities disagree on matters of detail, where regulation dress was never worn, or where the dress worn was never authorized. These are problems which experienced researchers will recognize and readily concede.

There is also the question of campaign dress. Up to the turn of the eighteenth century one went to war in full dress; but what of the twentieth? Shall we show full dress or service dress? Both are interesting, so examples of each are given.

The main concern, however, has been to include as many different nationalities as possible within the limited compass of the work, even at the expense, perhaps, of leaving out some events.

I am greatly indebted to the following authorities for the notes and sketches which they kindly sent me from time to time:

The late Wynard Aerts, of Brussels, on the Belgian Army; Mr. M. Canter, of Regina, Saskatchewan, on Mexican uniforms and the American Civil War; the late Mr. A. Lubimov, of Leningrad, on the Russian Army of Napoleonic times; Monsieur C. Tavard, of Paris, on various artillery uniforms; Major G. Tylden, E.D., on the Boer artillery; and Mr. W. Zweguintzow, of Paris, on Russian uniforms.

# CONTENTS

4    **Uniform Clothing: The Early Stages**

6    **The Great Northern War (1700–21)**

8    **The War of the Spanish Succession (1701–13)**

12    **The War of the Austrian Succession (1740–48)**

14    **The French and Indian War (1756–59)**

18    **The Seven Years War (1756–63)**

22    **The American Revolution (1775–78)**

28    **The Brabant Rebellion (1789)**

30    **The Napoleonic Wars (1803–12)**

48    **The War of 1812**

50    **The Struggles for Latin American Independence (1810–18)**

52    **The French Conquest of Algeria (1830–47)**

54    **The Mexican War (1846–48)**

56    **The 1848 Revolutions**

58    **The Crimean War (1854–56)**

68    **The Indian Mutiny (1858)**

74    **The Franco-Austrian War in Italy (1858–59)**

78    **The War of the Danish Duchies (1864)**

82    **The American Civil War (1861–65)**

90    **The Franco-German War (1870–71)**

98    **The Spanish-American War (1898)**

102    **The South African War (1899–1902)**

108    **The Boxer Rebellion (1900)**

116    **The Russo-Japanese War (1904–05)**

120    **The Italo-Turkish War (1911–12)**

122    **The Balkan Wars (1912–13)**

130    **World War I (1914–18)**

154    **Glossary**

156    **Places to Visit**

157    **Books to Read**

158    **Index**

## Uniform Clothing: The Early Stages

Although the color and design of military dress were not subject to regulation before the late seventeenth century, the principle of a uniform method of clothing dates from a much earlier age and stems from the natural result of buying cloth and similar materials in bulk.

In England, as in many other countries, sundry Royal Warrants from the Restoration onward specified the various colors of coats and facings to be worn by different units, until we come to the very detailed dress regulations of modern times.

In 1686, for example, the English 2nd Regiment of Foot was to wear a red coat lined in green, with green breeches and white stockings. In 1688, the 3rd Foot had the same, but with 'cross pockets with three scallops, and large plain pewter buttons'. If the artillerymen of England did not conform, it was merely because they were originally administered, not by the war department, but by the Board of Ordnance.

This explains the crimson uniform of the artillery matross shown here, since in

Pictured here are typical European military uniforms of the late seventeenth century. The private (*above*) is of the French Régiment de Piémont, 1690. On the opposite page are (*left*) a matross of the British Train of Artillery, 1695 and (*right*) a private of the Royal Regiment of Fuzileers, 1690. The matross is holding a linstock, a staff which held a lighted match for firing cannon.

4

those days the guns were not served by regular soldiers, but by a 'train' recruited solely for the duration of a campaign and dismissed at its conclusion. The issue of clothing, therefore, presumably followed the same principle.

The Fusiliers were raised primarily to act as escorts for the 'train', but eventually they found their place in the line as the 7th Foot. They were subsequently named 'My Royal Regiment of Fuzileers' and thereby acquired blue facings in place of the yellow originally worn.

The Piedmont Regiment of France was one of the senior infantry regiments of that country, wearing the very light gray (*gris-blanc*) coat which was continued until well into the eighteenth century.

## The Great Northern War (1700–21)

In 1699, a coalition against Sweden forced Charles XII to adopt an aggressive attitude on the principle that attack is the best means of defense. He struck accordingly, and having successfully disposed of the Danish menace, directed his attention to Russia, whose army he destroyed at the Narva on November 19, 1700.

Hostilities broke out again in 1707, when Charles marched from Saxony with an army of 24,000 horse and 20,000 foot soldiers to attack the Russians. The latter, however, in an early exercise of their 'scorched earth' policy, retreated before the invader, trusting— as in later campaigns—to the effects of the deadly Russian winter. As it happened, the winter of 1708 was the worst that Europe had known for a century, and in the following summer the sick and demoralized Swedish Army was virtually annihilated at Poltava.

Originally, the Swedish infantry wore coats of regimental colors—red, yellow, gray, green or blue, with cuffs in contrasting colors—but in 1690 a universal blue uniform was introduced. In

Swedish grenadier, 1700.

Charles XII's reign the various regiments were distinguished by breeches and stockings in their own particular colors, as well as by colored loops on the buttonholes. The grenadiers wore a brass mitre-cap with embossed devices of a regimental pattern. In the field, the officers were dressed in gray; waistcoats for all ranks continued to be made of leather.

The cavalry wore the regulation blue coat with heavy boots and the ubiquitous tricorne hat of the period, which was also the headdress for the battalion companies in the infantry.

On the Russian side, the uniforms conformed to the general style of the period, although at the beginning of Peter the Great's reign the color—in the infantry and dragoons at least—was left to the discretion of individual commanders.

For headdress, the infantry had the tricorne and grenadier cap, as well as a characteristic round cap, flat at the top, and provided with ear-flaps which could be turned up when they were not in use.

The war finally came to an end in 1721, in the reign of Charles' sister.

Russian dragoon, 1700.

## The War of the Spanish Succession (1701–13)

By the early eighteenth century military uniform was beginning to develop a distinctive character of its own. The hat, hitherto turned up more or less at the wearer's whim, was now cocked uncompromisingly in the three-cornered shape that was to endure for most of the century, and a greater uniformity became apparent in the leg-wear.

The coat was ample, with very wide cuffs which could be turned down in bad weather, and the waistbelt continued to be worn in a comfortable position low on the abdomen. Yet, although the officers, for their part, contrived to achieve a measure of smartness, the same could not be said for the men. Admittedly, the long hair was often cut short (at least on service), but the stockings were mostly ill-fitting and crumpled at the ankles; and the square-toed shoes, probably very uncomfortable in wear, were not made in left or right fittings, but to a single pattern for both feet. Nor, one feels, was personal cleanliness much encouraged.

In short, the common soldier was meant for fighting and not for show, and if the Duke of Marlborough recognized the value of morale, and looked after his troops accordingly, he was probably a pioneer in that departure.

The first Foot Guards were very much his favorites, for had he not joined the Regiment as an Ensign in 1667 and later become its Colonel? At Blenheim in 1704, the First Foot Guards were chosen to lead the attack on the Schellenberg.

A picture by Laguerre in Marlborough House, shows the Regiment fording a river, probably the Danube. The dress seems remarkable for its simplicity, although the grenadiers wear the typical mitre-cap with its blue cloth front and embroidered devices. The officers, curiously enough, are dressed in blue coats with gold lace and wear their hair long and powdered under a small tricorne.

The war of the Spanish Succession grew out of the rival claims to the Spanish throne of Louis XIV's grandson Philip and the Archduke Charles of Austria; while France backed by Spain and Bavaria naturally supported the former, the Archduke's cause was eagerly embraced by Great Britain, as well as Austria, as an opportunity to curb the power of the French king. Holland, Denmark and eventually Portugal also

Private, 1st Foot Guards, c. 1704.

Private, British line regiment, c. 1704.

9

Early eighteenth century uniforms of the French infantry. (*Left*) a private of the Regiment de Champagne and (*right*) a private of the Régiment Royal.

fought for the Archduke's cause.

Little pictorial evidence survives of the uniform of British line regiments at this time. They appear to have been clothed in the same style as the Guards, with the possible exception of the buttonhole loops. The coat remained red in all units, which were identified mainly by the color of their cuffs and linings, and sometimes by their breeches and stockings. The commanding officer's taste, rather than official regulations, probably had much to do with this.

In France, on the other hand, the picture was different. The troops wore silver-gray coats, with cuffs of the same color, or in some cases, in regimental colors (mostly blue or red). Buttons were either brass or white metal, but the chief distinction lay in the patterns of the pocket-flaps.

Thus the Regiment de Champagne, shown here, had double vertical pockets, with six brass buttons set in pairs on each flap, and four buttons on each cuff. Picardie (the senior line regiment in the French Army) wore the same, except that the pocket-flaps had nine brass buttons each, set in threes to form three triangles with the apex pointing to the front of the garment, and the cuffs had only three buttons. In both regiments the corners of the flaps were rounded and the edges straight.

Among the Austrians was a Walloon regiment, for the Netherlands, at that time, were part of the Austrian Empire. The green coat was unusual for an Imperial-and-Royal unit, but was worn in all the eight Netherlandish regiments which were then in the Austrian service.

In 1708, all infantry regiments based in metropolitan Austria-Hungary received 'pearl-white' coats, the units being identified by the color of their cuffs, linings, waistcoats, breeches and stockings. At the same time, the bandsmen were ordered to wear reversed colors (for example, red coats with white cuffs where the troops wore white coats with red cuffs), a distinction which, rather surprisingly, was shared by the noncommissioned officers. Officers did not go into uniform until about 1718, and it would seem that in the early stages they too wore reversed uniform colors.

Private, Walloon Regiment, Austrian Infantry, 1707. (*Below*) Grenadier cap of the same regiment.

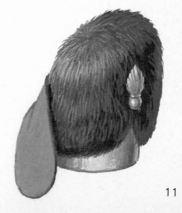

11

De Ligne Dragoon, Austrian Army, c. 1748. (*Opposite*) privates, British 13th Foot and French Régiment du Roy, c. 1745.

### The War of the Austrian Succession (1740–48)

At the death of the Hapsburg Emperor Charles VI in 1740, the inevitable international quarrels arose over the election of his successor. At Warsaw, on January 8, 1745, the Quadruple Alliance—Great Britain, Austria, Holland and Saxony—was formed as a counter to the menacing attitude of the French.

The immediate object of the French army was to cover the siege of Tournai. Louis XV and the Dauphin came to watch the operations, which opened at Fontenoy with that legendary and much discussed piece of bravado, '*Tirez les premiers, Messieurs les Anglais*'. Fortescue informs us that the British line fired, killing fifty officers and 760 men of the three foremost French regiments, with the Regiment du Roy alone losing thirty-seven officers and 345 men at the hands of the 2nd Regiment of Foot Guards.

The presence of the Royal party did much for French morale: the tireless Maurice de Saxe himself, though ill, did

not hesitate to mount his horse and collect cavalry for a charge. Further artillery was then brought up, and in one tremendous blow the battle was won for France.

By this period, the coat skirts were turned back to facilitate marching. Stockings—most inadequate in bad weather and muddy conditions—were now protected by gaiters reaching above the knee. The coat remained ample (it was, in fact, the equivalent of a modern overcoat, since a sleeved waistcoat was worn underneath), and the turned-over lapels usually showed a lining in the same color as the cuffs. In most armies, this color denoted the regiment.

The French Army, still wearing the traditional silver-gray followed the same broad pattern, with the additional regimental distinctions of pockets and buttons.

The Austrian regiment of de Ligne's Dragoons was a Walloon unit which later made a name for itself as Vincent's and Latour's, and of which the Belgians are still justly proud.

13

## The French and Indian War (1756-59)

In the early seventeenth century, colonization of the North American continent had been undertaken by the French and English almost simultaneously. As time went on, the British became firmly established in such territories as Virginia, Maryland, the Carolinas and New York (named after the Duke of York, later James II). The French were concentrated in Louisiana, Michigan, Illinois and Canada.

Ill-feeling between France and England soon broke out into petty skirmishing, resulting in a full-fledged attack shortly after the War of the Spanish Succession. The campaign was short, but it initiated that long-drawn out conflict which occurred off and on in North America until the early nineteenth century.

The 60th Foot was raised in New York in 1755 under the title of The Royal American Regiment. Originally a normal line unit, it later became the first of the British rifle regiments, The King's Royal Rifle Corps: a strange conversion occasioned by the fact that its 5th Battalion was

British Marine, 1756, and the Marine cap (*above*).

Privates, British 60th Foot and Roger's Rangers, 1757.

trained entirely for skirmishing and clothed accordingly in dark green. The experiment proved so successful that the whole regiment was eventually equipped for a 'rifle' role.

The value of experienced backwoodsmen became increasingly evident in wooded country quite unsuitable for the mass deployments characteristic of the period. Both sides employed Indians, but the French also had their *coureurs des bois,* the British answer to which was numerous corps of irregular rangers raised from the local inhabitants. Of these, Roger's is one of the most famous.

These departures, of course, did not deprive the existing line regiments of their own light companies, nor of the grenadier companies which acted as shock troops. The grenadier retained the mitre-cap, which had originally been

15

designed as a more stable headdress than the conventional hat. In the British Army, at this period, these caps were mostly red, with a tall front in the regimental facing color bearing the Royal Cypher, while the little flap displayed the White Horse of Hanover on a red ground, with the motto 'NEC ASPERA TERRENT' above.

One of the outstanding actions of the war was General James Wolfe's famous victory on the Plains of Abraham, at Quebec, on September 13, 1759. The battle was a typical example of a surprise attack in unexpected quarters, and the episode of the boatloads of soldiers, being rowed silently up river at dead of night, is a classic of its kind.

The Royal Sussex Regiment proudly display a white plume in their badge. This, they tell us, is to commemorate their victory at Quebec when, as the 35th Foot, they took the plumes from the opposing French Regiment's headdresses. But no

French Orléans Dragoon and private of the Royal Roussillon Regiment, 1758.

French record reveals the presence of a white plume on the hats of the Royal Roussillon Regiment.

However, one hesitates to completely disregard the story. It often happened that a commanding officer would order his regiment to wear some distinguishing mark when the uniform could lend itself to confusion. Oak leaves were frequently used, but in the case of Royal Roussillon it is possible that white feathers were available and adapted for that purpose.

The uniform did, in fact, bear a close resemblance to the Régiment de la Sarre, with its blue cuffs and brass buttons, the only difference being that, while La Sarre had round-cornered pocket-flaps, Roussillon's were pointed; and La Sarre's three buttons on the cuffs were replaced by six in Roussillon.

The sixteen regiments, of which Orléans Dragoons was numbered 7th, were distinguished not only by the color of their cuffs and waistcoats, but also by the pattern on the border edging the saddle-cloth and holster-caps.

British Grenadier caps. (*From the top*) 44th Foot, 42nd Foot, 27th Foot, 48th Foot and 46th Foot.

Officers of the
British 11th Dragoons
and 24th Foot, 1756.

### The Seven Years War (1756–63)

In the second half of the eighteenth century, military uniforms were beginning to lose some of their heaviness, especially in the Prussian Army. Frederick II took a great interest in his troops—his nickname of *der alte Fritz* denoted affection rather than derision—and he was probably personally responsible for many of the innovations which were made in their dress.

The infantry regiments, as in other countries, each had its own grenadier and light companies, but in Prussia the light company was known as fusiliers and the main body were classed as musketeers. At this period they were distinguished by their headdress, the musketeers wearing the conventional tricorne, the grenadiers a tall mitre-cap with a metal front, and the fusiliers a small metal-fronted cap, something like a miniature mitre-cap with a pointed ornament at the top. Perhaps this was a fore-runner of the famous pickelhaube. One is tempted to think so, although there is no evidence to that effect.

The need for light cavalry was beginning to manifest itself at this period, and many countries were raising regiments of hussars on the Hungarian model. The uniform was always based on Hungarian national costume, and the very name is derived from the Hungarian word *huszár,* meaning the 'twentieth man' and denoting the one man in twenty who was picked by ballot for service in the Hungarian army.

The growing menace of Frederick the Great's Prussia was causing concern in Europe, with the result that yet another coalition came into being, consisting of Austria, France, Russia, Sweden and Saxony. This formidable opposition did not deter the Prussian king, and he struck first, marching to the Saxon frontier on August 29, 1756, and proving the wisdom of his move by beating the Austrians and Saxons before the year was out.

Prussian private of the Regiment von Schwerin, 1757

In 1759 British troops were sent to Frederick's assistance, and on August 1 the famous battle of Minden took place. Minden was one of the major British successes in this war—the battle which is still remembered in six infantry regiments when they wear roses in their hats on Minden Day to commemorate the action of the 12th, 20th, 23rd, 25th, 37th and 51st Regiments of Foot. Tommy Atkins was not yet born, but his ancestors already displayed his cheery optimism as they advanced under fire through the rose gardens of Minden, picking the blooms and decking their hats in jaunty defiance.

As in earlier wars, there were red-coated regiments of Irish and Swiss in the French service. One of these Swiss units—Diesbach's—fought at Rossbach, on November 3, 1757, with such bravery that it earned the admiration of the Great Frederick himself. The battle was already lost for the French, but

(*Above*) fusilier cap, 40th Prussian Infantry Regiment, 1757, and (*right*) 8th Prussian Hussars, 1758.

the Swiss refused to give in. Curious, the King of Prussia asked, 'What are those red brick walls which my artillery cannot breach?' On being told their identity, the King remained silent, then slowly raised his hat, deeply moved by their steadfast devotion.

The faithfulness of the Swiss, in any service, is proverbial: and it is appropriate here to dispel the notion of the 'Swiss mercenary'. The facts are given concisely by Captain de Vallière in his book *'Honneur et Fidélité'*, for this is what he writes: 'The Swiss regiments were fully operational units which Switzerland lent to France. The Cantons had the right to recall their troops when necessary. This was a very special arrangement, supervised officially by the contracting states, and had nothing to do with the individual recruiting of mercenaries'.

French infantry privates: Touraine Regiment and Swiss Régiment de Diesbach.

Officer, British 15th
Foot, 1776.

## The American Revolution (1775–78)

For some time a feeling of unrest had prevailed among the North American colonists, owing chiefly to a mishandling of their problems by the British Government and their representatives in the colonies. The last straw was the imposition of a tax of three-pence on every pound of tea, when the colonists were being denied a representative voice in the policies with which they were directly concerned. On December 16, 1773, 340 chests of tea were seized by the inhabitants of Boston and thrown overboard.

A kind of uneasy truce ensued. The colonists were purposely disregarding the order to surrender their arms, and in April, 1775 a British detachment was sent to Concord to seize a store of weapons. On the way it passed through the village of Lexington, where it encountered a small party of enraged colonists. A single individual recklessly fired his musket, thereby sparking off the war which led to independence.

In the following month, on May 10, Fort Ticonderoga was taken by the Americans, but British reinforcements were now landing at Boston.

The colonists were now in open rebellion, and George Washington was appointed commander-in-chief of their forces in June.

The war, developing as it did in wooded country profusely interspersed with tortuous water-courses, was definitely an infantryman's business—and light infantry at that. Yet no operation can proceed without mounted troops wherever the terrain is suitable, and light dragoons seemed the most appropriate for the conditions prevailing in North America.

Light cavalry was more or less in its infancy, at least in Great Britain. The hussars which were forming in other countries did not appear in the British Army until the end of the century, but light dragoons had been in existence for some years. Of these, the 16th and 17th were chosen for service in North America.

Both regiments wore the elegant light cavalry helmet of the period, with its short crimson 'mane' falling over the right side. The 17th wore white facings; the 16th, blue. The Death's Head badge is reputed to have been given to the 17th on its formation by its first commanding officer, who wished to commemorate

Royal Artillery gunner, 1777.

the death of General Wolfe at Quebec in 1759, but the origin of the device may actually be far older.

The general appearance of the light dragoon officer's uniform reveals the continuing trend for the garments to shed their former cumbersome fullness: coats now fitted closer to the body, cuffs and lapels became narrower and sleeves were tighter.

The Royal Regiment of Artillery, firmly established on a permanent basis for over sixty years, continued to appear in the traditional blue coat which it has worn ever since. It was still administered by the Board of Ordnance, and its badge was the Ordnance Arms. In dress, it followed the pattern of the Army, at this period governed by the 1768 Clothing Warrant.

In 1777, gunners' hats were to have a gold lace, but it seems likely that the troops on service in North America continued to wear a plain, or black-laced hat. The 4th Battalion, at this period, was authorized, for some unknown reason, to wear a

Officer of the
British 17th Light
Dragoons, 1775.

A private of
the Hessian Regiment Erbprinz.
1776.

black feather in their hats.

The waistcoat and breeches, which had been buff until 1768, were now white. The hair was powdered and 'clubbed' (i.e. turned up at the neck and tied, instead of hanging down the back). Needless to say, little powdering was done on active service, although commanding officers would see that their men's hair was kept tidy.

A portrait of an officer of the 15th Foot, on the other hand, shows him hatless and with hair carefully dressed and powdered; obviously painstakingly prepared for the occasion. The 15th was very active in America, and the officer's coat shows the yellow collar, lapels and cuffs proper to the Regiment. The buttons and loops, set in pairs, are silver. The stock, waistcoat and breeches are correctly shown as white, while the sash, until lately worn over the right shoulder, now encircles the waist, and in this case appears to be twisted corkscrew fashion. The hat would very likely have a silver lace around the edge to conform with the silver loops on the coat, and the cockade would certainly be black.

A number of Hessian troops was employed by the British,

at a cost of over £3,000,000 to the Exchequer. Their blue uniforms sometimes caused confusion in their similarity, at a distance, to the Americans'; they were good soldiers, and two regiments— von Knyphausen's and von Lossberg's—became famous.

Naturally enough, in the early stages of the war, the Americans paid little attention to the question of uniform. Arms and ammunition were the main concern, yet clothing had eventually to be provided. Many local corps were formed and dressed in as near an approach to uniform as could be supplied.

One such body was the famous 'Green Mountain Boys', formed in 1770 in what is today Vermont to protect the rights of settlers against the claims of New York officials to ownership of their land. They took part in the Fort Ticonderoga battle in 1775, led by their founder Ethan Allen. Later, under Seth Warner, they were sent to the Army of the North. They achieved a notable victory at Bennington in 1777, during the Saratoga Campaign, a turning point in the war.

The 1st New York Regiment (McDougall's) was

(*Above*) American Green Mountain Boys, private, 1776, and (*below*) British light infantry helmet (5th Foot), c. 1775. (*Opposite*) American troops, 1775: private, 1st New York Regiment and officer, Rhode Island Artillery.

typical of the American infantry, with its dark blue coat and red facings. The cut of the garments and much of the equipment resembled the British pattern, but in many cases thick woollen stockings were worn with short black gaiters. For summer wear, there was a preference for long white pantaloons, shaped like gaiters in the lower leg, and buttoned over the footwear.

Although a national corps of artillery existed, dressed very much like its British counterpart in blue coats with red facings, the principle of local bodies of artillery was by no means discouraged. Thus, we find the inhabitants of Rhode Island raising a force of gunners clothed in brown, with red facings. The breeches were buff, and the headdress appears to have been a curious kind of blue cap of a nautical appearance further enhanced by the addition of an anchor badge on the front.

27

The colorful uniforms of two of the military units formed by local patriots during the rebellion in Brabant. The officer of the Ypres Volunteers (*left*) has the Belgian colors in his plume and cockade. (*Above*) the uniform of the St. Christopher Volunteers, a Brussels unit.

## The Brabant Rebellion (1789)

Revolution was in the air as the eighteenth century drew to its close. The success of the American colonists' venture may have prompted other liberal minds in Europe to attempt similar action, especially in view of the friendship which had sprung up between France and the United States—a logical conclusion to the help which the French had given the Americans.

In 1789, the Belgian province of Brabant was under Austrian rule, as part of the Netherlands. The people, however, enjoyed certain inherited rights which they were anxious to preserve, and when the Emperor Joseph II attempted to infringe upon these rights, trouble was bound to ensue. The news from France was sufficient incentive, and very soon undisguised revolution broke out, led by Henry Van der Noot.

As usual, thousands of local patriots formed themselves into sundry military units, each with its own uniform, but all marching under the colors which have since become those of the national flag of Belgium—black, yellow and red. These are based upon the heraldic arms of the Province: black for the field of the blazon, yellow for the Lion of Brabant and red for its tongue and claws.

The uniforms, fortunately, were recorded on the spot by an artist whose work may still be seen in the Royal Army Museum in Brussels—a remarkable collection of very detailed paintings.

On the whole, the pattern is French in character, particularly in the cut of the garments and the wearing of epaulettes in the French manner by the officers. Thus, the Ypres Volunteers, for example, could easily be mistaken for French infantry of the period were it not for their black lapels and the Belgian colors in their plume and cockade.

The same might be said of the Tongerloo Dragoons, but here the cuff is of a very distinctive pattern, which is repeated, incidentally, in the Brussels Volunteers. It was not usual, at this period, to find troops wearing pointed cuffs with a central cuff-slash bearing a row of buttons. The conventional design, where buttons were included, was to sew these on a rectangular upright slash covering a square cuff.

The country was liberated on December 17, 1789. The following day Van der Noot and his staff made their triumphal entry into Brussels after only six weeks fighting.

## The Napoleonic Wars (1803–12)

The paradox of the French Revolution is that, far from initiating a long era of popular government, it produced — and very soon, at that — not only a reversion to a sovereign's rule, but a pure and uncompromising Empire.

When Napoleon Bonaparte crowned himself as Napoleon I, *Empereur des Français,* in 1804, one can but suppose that France, weakened by ideological quarrels, looked forward with relief to a period of stable government under a purposeful leader.

Unfortunately, the new monarch's idea of achieving stability was to render the rest of Europe incapable of molesting him: a splendid idea if only others will cooperate. But inevitably, the outcome could only result in a series of wars — long and tedious wars which lasted virtually as long as the first French Empire itself.

In these, Great Britain played an important part, both in the political and in the military fields. The British Army had been in a state of alert since the outbreak of the Revolution in 1789. This was the first time for centuries that a powerful European monarch had been deposed,

and public opinion in England—probably still recalling its own Carolean regicide—promptly regarded France as the archenemy.

At the turn of the century, the British Army had discarded the long-tailed coat in favor of a short jacket with a high standing collar, short tails and, instead of lapels, a system of buttonholes looped in regimental lace and set in singles or pairs according to regiment. A further distinction occurred in the shape of these loops, which could be square-ended, pointed or 'bastion'-shaped (i.e. pointed, but with incurving sides in the form of a pike-head).

The hat had become larger, and two-cornered in shape, while the gaiters now reached just below the knee. Very soon, however, the hat was exchanged for a cylindrical shako—the 'stove-pipe cap' made of lacquered material at first, but replaced by one of felt in 1806.

In light infantry regiments, the cap was conical in shape, with a green plume and bugle-horn badge in front. Rifle regiments were clothed in very dark green, with red facings for the 60th and black for the 95th.

The Household Cavalry and dragoons wore a handsome leather helmet with a comb of classical design and a long streamer of black horsehair hanging down the back. The one exception was the 2nd Dragoons—The Royal Scots Greys— who had the bearskin cap which is still worn today.

The light dragoons, now a well-established branch of the Army, wore dark blue jackets, profusely laced in gold or silver, and 'Tarleton' helmets—a hard leather headdress with a colored turban.

This was also the type of helmet worn by the Royal Horse

Private, British 13th Light Dragoons, 1814.

Artillery, that new branch formed in 1793 to provide fast-moving guns for the cavalry. Indeed, on one famous occasion, the Horse Artillery carried out a specifically cavalry action, when Captain Norman Ramsay's Troop, at full gallop 'with horses stretching like greyhounds over the plain' (Napier) charged the enemy at Fuentes de Oñoro on May 5, 1811, guns and limbers bounding behind in a headlong cavalcade.

The field artillery, in conformity with the usual practice, wore an infantry-pattern uniform, but in blue instead of red.

The queued hair, which had been in force for so long, was abolished on August 1, 1808, much to the relief of the troops; and in 1811 a new type of shako was authorized: the 'Belgic' cap of Waterloo fame.

This was issued to the infantry of the line and the foot artillery, and consisted of a black felt crown 6¾ inches high fitted with an 8¼-inch false front.

The light infantry continued to wear their conical caps, but a complete change occurred in the light dragoons. A shako, bell-topped and of French appearance, now replaced the hel-

Trooper, The Life Guards, 1815 and sergeant, Royal Horse Artillery, 1815.

French Army uniforms. A chasseur of the Guard and (*right*) a
trumpeter, 16th Dragoons, 1812.

met; and the laced jacket was discarded for a simpler but more
colorful version resembling a Polish *kurtka*. This was a short-
tailed jacket, with broad lapels, collar, cuffs and turnbacks
in the regimental facing color, bearing fringed epaulettes in
either yellow or white, according to the metal in which the
buttons were made.

Although lancers had not yet found their place in the British
Army, hussars were now becoming a popular branch of the
light cavalry. The 7th, 10th, 15th and 18th Light Dragoons
were converted to hussars and clothed in the truly resplendent
uniforms of that branch—dark blue jackets with lavish braiding of gold or silver, elaborate pelisses with the same display of
splendor, and the curious 'mirliton'—a tall peakless conical

French Cavalry, 1815. 4th Hussars and (*right*) trooper, 11th
Cuirassiers.

cap, wound around with a colored silk streamer. This was
later replaced by the conventional hussar busby, worn with a
colored bag and plume.

On the French side, the pattern was unexpectedly conserv-
ative. Admittedly, the white coats symbolizing the *Ancien
Régime* had been supplanted by the blue ones of the National
Guard; but the general effect of the costume, with its wide
expanse of waistcoat and long coattails, was very much that
of the 1780's.

In the infantry of the line, the lapels were normally white,
piped in red at the edges. The breeches were also white, but
worn with long gaiters (black in winter and white in summer)
reaching above the knee. For headdress, the bell-topped shako

French head-dresses 1815. Carabinier's helmet, Polish czapka and helmet of dragoons of the Guard.

was the normal wear, although the felt bicorne typical of the Revolutionary period was used extensively on active service.

In the light infantry, on the other hand, things were different. The uniform was basically blue throughout, but the gaiters were of the short variety, reaching half-way up the calf, while the jacket was short-tailed with white metal buttons, as opposed to the brass ones of the line.

The infantry of the Guard consisted mainly of grenadiers and chasseurs—both dressed very much alike in bearskin caps and blue coats, the main difference being that the grenadiers wore a copper (not brass) plate on the bearskin, while the chasseurs had none.

The chief cavalry branches were the cuirassiers, carabiniers, dragoons, chasseurs, hussars and lancers, of which the dragoons, chasseurs and lancers each contributed one regiment for the Guard. It will be recalled, incidentally, that Napoleon's favorite attire was the familiar undress coat of a colonel of the *chasseurs à cheval* of the Guard. The Guard also included such troops as horse grenadiers and *gendarmes d'élite;*

French troops 1815. (*Left to right*) foot artillery gunner, light infantry cornet, and corporal, infantry of the line.

and it naturally had its own artillery, which consisted of horse
and foot units.

The horse artillery was dressed hussar-fashion in blue with
red facings and lacing, and wore a large busby with a red bag
and plume. The horses were uniformly black. In the foot
branch, the uniform was entirely blue with red facings, but
here the headdress was the grenadier bearskin fitted with a
leather peak over the eyes.

The artillery of the line was dressed somewhat similarly
to the guard, except for the headdress, which took the form
of the regulation bell-topped shako in both the horse and the
foot branches of this arm of service.

Dragoon officer,
Austrian Army,
1805.

The cuirassiers wore the classical-type helmet with a long black horsehair streamer at the back and the distinctive steel cuirass which gave them their name. The coat was blue with collar, cuffs and turnbacks in regimental colors.

The same type of helmet, but in brass, was worn by the dragoons. The coat, however, was green, and here the regiments were distinguished by the color of the collar, lapels and cuffs, and also by the set of the pocket-flaps (i.e. whether vertical or horizontal).

The carabiniers, of which there were two regiments, were first dressed grenadier-fashion, with bearskin caps and blue coats, but on December 24, 1809 an entirely new uniform was authorized, consisting of a large dragoon-type helmet decorated with an impressive scarlet crest, a white coat with light blue facings and a brass cuirass. Scarlet epaulettes completed this very resplendent ensemble.

The
artillery gunners (*below*) are
wearing the uniform colors—
brown coat with red facings—
which were to be retained
until 1914.

The chasseurs wore green, with different facing colors according to regiments, and the regulation bell-topped shako; but in the hussars every regiment was clothed differently. The headdress was the normal shako, except in the elite companies, where it was replaced by the busby. This distinction also applied to the same companies in the chasseurs as well as to the Guard regiment of that arm. Indeed, the latter unit resembled a hussar regiment rather than chasseurs, since they wore a green jacket laced in bright yellow, and a scarlet pelisse.

The lancers were also called *chevaulégers,* or light horse. In the line, there were six regiments, wearing green coats with regimental facings and carabinier-type helmets with a black crest. In the Guard, however, the lancers were a Polish regiment, dressed in blue with crimson facings. A second Guard regiment was added later, drawn from the former Dutch Army, and clothed in scarlet. Both units wore the distinctive Polish lance-cap.

The Austrian infantry at this time was wearing the traditional white uniform which was to remain until

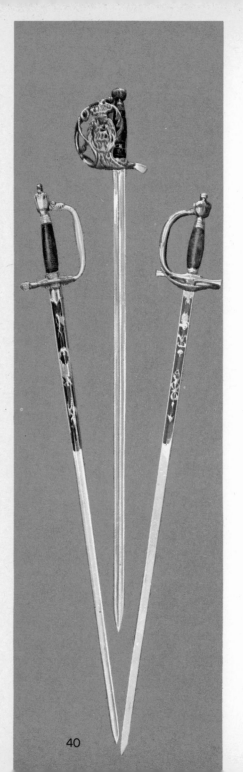

the latter half of the next
century, with regimental facing colors displayed on the
collar, cuffs and turnbacks.
By a system of subtle differences in the tone of the
colors, it was possible to
dress every regiment differently, especially as the 'Germans' had white breeches
and the Hungarians had blue.

For many years the artil-
lery had worn brown coats
with red facings, and they
continued to do so until 1914.
But the cavalry, with its
various branches, presented
a much more colorful ap-
pearance. The cuirassiers
wore the white coat and a
blackened steel breast-plate
(no back-plate) with a black
helmet surmounted by a brass
comb supporting a black-
over-yellow crest. The facing
color appeared on the collar-
patch, cuffs and one-inch
edging of the turnbacks.

The lancers, of whom there
were four regiments, were
dressed in green uniforms of
Polish design: two regiments
in dark green and two in
'grass green'. The facings of
the tunic were red for all four
regiments.

The hussar uniform pro-
vided ample opportunity for
no two regiments to be dressed alike; but in the dragoon

branch a considerable amount of confusion arose when some chevauléger regiments were ordered to exchange their green coats for white, and some dragoons, hitherto 'white', became 'green'.

In 1806 the stout leather helmet was discarded and a bell-topped headdress taken into wear, one of the earliest examples of a shako fitted with a peak back and front. This rear peak was imitated in other armies and remained in wear, in such countries as Switzerland, Denmark and Sweden, until the time of World War I over a century later.

The Austrian grenadiers' bearskin cap was a very distinctive article, of a typical design found nowhere else. It can perhaps best be described as a peaked bearskin, carrying a large frontal brass plate, but with much of the top and back removed to leave a kind of voluminous fur cap with a large upright front around the plate. The cutaway back part was covered with cloth in the regimental facing color, with lines of lace.

In Russia, the basic color, at all events for the infantry and artillery, was a fairly dark green, and the head-

41

dress was the ubiquitous bell-topped shako. In the early stages of the Napoleonic Wars, this was of standard design, but in 1812 it was altered to a different shape in which the top, hitherto flat and level, was now incurved in the middle, to rise at the back and front.

In the infantry, the collar and cuffs were scarlet for all units, and the regiments in a division were designated by the color of the shoulder-straps (which carried the divisional number). The 1st regiment wore scarlet; the 2nd, white; the 3rd, yellow; and the 4th green with red piping.

The Russian cavalry was particularly splendid, and included such bodies as cuirassiers, dragoons, hussars, lancers, and of course the famous Cossacks which were truly the national cavalry of the Empire. The regular cavalry branches were dressed in the conventional style of the period, much influenced, seemingly, by the Prussian pattern; but the Cossacks

Russian troops. (*Left*) officer, Don Cossacks, c. 1812, and (*right*) a grenadier, c. 1808.

42

had their own traditional dress.

It may come as a surprise to learn that they even had a full-dress uniform, although whether this was much worn is a matter for conjecture. Thus, the Ukrainian Cossacks, for instance, of whom there were four regiments, wore short blue jackets and khaki trousers, with the regimental facing color shown on the collar, cuffs, trouser-band and busby-bag. The Ural Cossacks had long blue coats and trousers with a double crimson band, and the Cossacks of the Bug had an all-blue uniform with white facings. Even two regiments of Kalmucks are recorded as having a dress uniform consisting of a black fur lance-cap with a square yellow top, and a blue coat and trousers with red piping and trouser-bands. The Prussian uniforms bore a strong resemblance to the Russian, except that they were blue instead of green.

The Prussian Army was virtually annihilated at Jena and Auerstadt in 1806, but until then the infantry consisted of sixty regiments distinguished by a combination of facing colors and buttons. Later, however, in the 1809 reorganization, the system was much simplified, whereby the facing color (collar and cuffs) denoted the province (e.g. East Prussia, red; West Prussia, crimson; Pomerania, white; Silesia, yellow). Within each province the regiments were identified by the color of the shoulder-straps, as follows: 1st regiment, white; 2nd, red; 3rd, yellow; and 4th, light blue.

According to the Dress Regulations of October 23, and October 26, 1808, the shako was to be bell-topped and seven inches high. For the grenadiers it carried a brass eagle plate and a monumental black plume, while the musketeers had the royal cyper in brass, and the fusiliers a large white and black cockade. In addition, the officers' shako was decorated with a small eagle badge at the side.

Later, Great Britain supplied much of the clothing to assist the rebirth of the Prussian Army, hence the great resemblance of the Silesian jägers and their British counterparts of the Rifle regiments.

The cavalry included regiments of cuirassiers in white and dragoons in light blue. Hussars were in various colors and uhlans (lancers) were in dark blue. The latter troops had been in existence in Prussia since 1740 and were recruited mainly

German troops. (*Left to right*) Silesian jäger, 1815; grenadier, 2nd Pomeranian Regiment, 1810; gunner, Württemberg Guard Artillery, 1812.

from the Polish provinces to the east of the country.

Every one of the German states had its own army, and after the 1806 defeats, most of the states found it expedient to come over to the French side, bringing a tremendous influx of manpower to the Napoleonic ambitions. A strong contingent from Baden, for instance, fought in the Peninsula, where they wore blue uniforms of either German or French appearance, according to available supplies. Adequate clothing was a problem, and we find that a Baden regimental band, in need of new headgear, simply made use of some helmets abandoned by the British 23rd Light Dragoons after the battle of Talavera on March 28, 1809.

Bavaria was a frequent, if not traditional ally of France in many continental wars. The uniform of this period was mostly light blue in the infantry, white in the heavy cavalry and green in the light cavalry, while the hussars and lancers wore dark blue and green, respectively.

In Württemberg the basic color was dark blue with regimental facing colors on the collar, cuffs, turnbacks and, from about 1800 to 1813, the lapels as well. The cavalry consisted of dragoons in blue and light cavalry in green. Two complete sets of uniforms are preserved in the Military Museum at Rastatt: one of the Württemberg Light Infantry Regiment No. 9 (light green with black facings) and the other of the artillery of the Guard (light blue with black facings).

The Portuguese deserve mention here, especially in view of their activity in the Peninsular War. The infantry of the line wore dark blue jackets and trousers, with a tall-fronted shako which could well have been the prototype of the British 'Belgic' shako.

However, the better-known units were the *Caçadores* or light infantry, wearing the brown jackets that have since come to signify Portuguese troops in the popular mind. In 1809 a new uniform was introduced, with black facings, lacing and a conical cap to replace the tall-fronted shako first issued.

The Dutch-Belgians took an active part in the battle of Waterloo, with regiments of heavy and light cavalry, as well as infantry of the line, chasseurs, and artillery. The heavy cavalry consisted of two regiments of carabiniers (one Dutch and one Belgian) dressed in dark blue with red facings and a handsome steel helmet with brass fittings and a black crest.

The infantry of the line had a blue uniform and a shako (truly Belgic in this event) very similar to the British and Portuguese versions. The chasseurs, or light infantry, wore green coats with primrose facings and a bell-topped shako with a rear peak, which was also that of the artillery. The latter, however, were clothed in blue, with red facings.

Under Frederick Augustus, Duke of Warsaw, the Polish Army was reorganized on French lines, except in the fifteen lancer regiments which retained their traditional Polish dress of dark blue with different colored facings to distinguish each of the regiments.

The Polish square-topped *czapka* was worn in the infantry as well as in the lancers, but in the former case mostly by the *voltigeurs,* or light companies. The battalion companies wore the conventional bell-topped shako, and the grenadiers wore the French-pattern bearskin cap with its brass plate. The jacket was dark blue.

The chasseurs à cheval, or light horse, were dressed in green; the hussars were in dark blue with crimson facings;

Portuguese caçador, 1812, and Belgian carabinier, 1815.

A private of the 8th
Polish Lancers and a
Spanish infantry private,
the Queen's Regiment,
1806.

the 14th Cuirassiers in French uniforms. The remainder
formed the uhlans, or lancer branch. The artillery wore
dark green with black facings piped red in both the horse
and foot branches.

The white of the Spanish Army recalled the French
uniforms of the *Ancien Régime,* but in 1812 the infantry
adopted a dark blue coat for all regiments, with gray trousers
and a conical cap of British light infantry pattern, while
the dragoons were some of the few troops to wear yellow
as the basic color of their uniform coats.

47

## The War of 1812

England and France both wanted United States assistance in their own war against each other, which the United States, deeply involved in its own internal problems, refused to provide to either side. In retaliation Britain began impounding American sailors on the high seas, claiming they were escaped British sailors. At the same time, the United States was trying to extend its boundaries into Canada, adding additional friction to the already tense situation. Relations gradually worsened, and war was finally declared on June 18th.

The British Army took to the field in the regulation field service dress of the day: the 'Belgic' shako (where it had been issued), red jacket and blue-gray trousers.

On the other hand, the United States had by now developed a new uniform, more in keeping with contemporary costume. At the start of the campaign the coats were uniformly blue, with scarlet collars and cuffs, and there seems to have been no distinctions of facing colors between the regiments. In the main, the cut and lacing closely resembled the British design, and regimental designations appeared on buttons and cap-plate only.

British troops. (*Top*) field officer, 49th Foot; (*bottom*) bandsman, 1st Foot.

48

Platoon officers and other ranks wore a jacket very similar to the British except for color, while the field officers had a long-tailed coat, also of blue. The cap, cylindrical in shape, carried a version of plate and plume much larger than the British models. The plume was eight inches high for officers and six for other ranks.

Various peculiarities of manufacture are to be noted. Thus, the sleeves of the jacket were usually much too long, to allow for shrinkage. By the late summer of 1812, it became more difficult to obtain white material for the soldier's vests, and these, therefore, appeared in a variety of colors, such as gray or even drab. Rank distinctions were shown by the epaulettes—silver for officers and white for noncommissioned officers.

In customary tradition, the drummers' uniform was far more elaborate and colorful since it embodied the principle of 'reversed colors'. In this case, therefore, a drummer would wear a red coat with blue facings with regulation breeches or pantaloons.

American troops. (*Top*) infantry private; (*bottom*) light artillery sergeant.

49

## Struggles for Latin American Independence (1810–18)

By the time the Napoleonic Wars had ended, revolt was gaining ground in the American possessions of Spain and Portugal. The Spanish territories, particularly, far too vast to be administered adequately by a weakened home government thousands of miles away, were beginning to feel that they could manage their own affairs.

In Mexico, for instance, the first intimation was a tentative suggestion, at the turn of the eighteenth century, for the creation of three Spanish-American Kingdoms under the Crown of Spain. This was rejected, and various revolutionary governments thereafter ruled the country, with all the attendant strife. Any army uniforms that happened to be worn do not appear to have been subject to consistent regulation.

Dress of the Mexican militia (*left*) and the Mexican Grenadiers of Toluca.

Argentine 'infernale'

At the other end of the continent, the Argentines pro-
claimed their independence on May 25, 1810, and led by
San Martin and Belgrano, defeated the Spanish forces at
Chacabuco in 1817 and Maipu in 1818. San Martin then
led his victorious troops into Peru and occupied Lima on
June 9, 1821.

This was where the Argentine *infernales,* the red-coated
devil-riders of the plains, acquired their fame as light cavalry.
Whether or not their clothing was a regulation uniform
remains problematical, since few authorities have been able
to agree on the subject.

French infantrymen, c. 1830. Line regiment and Chasseurs d'Orléans.

### The French Conquest of Algeria (1830–47)

We have now come to the time when the French soldier began to wear the red trousers which later became so distinctive a part of his attire: an outcome, we are told, of the necessity for finding a commercial use for the red madder dye then being produced extensively in the French territories in North Africa.

The French conquest of Algeria grew out of a long-standing quarrel with the Dey of Algiers over corn supplied to France during the Directorate. French troops landed at Sidi-Ferruch on June 14, 1830, capturing Algiers on July 5. It was not until December 23, 1847 that the legendary Arab leader Abd-el-Kader finally surrendered to General Lamoricière.

The French infantry of the line—still sub-divided into grenadiers, battalion companies and voltigeurs—had retained a style of dress much resembling the Napoleonic, with its

Private, French Foreign Legion, 1832.

bell-topped shako and long-tailed coat.

By the 1840's, however, a new branch of light infantry had come into existence: the Chasseurs d'Orléans, clothed in dark blue with blue-gray trousers. They eventually replaced the existing *Infanterie légère* and, under the new denomination of Chasseurs à Pied, continued to wear basically the same uniform until 1914.

The Foreign Legion needs no introduction. This remarkable corps owed its origin to the eight foreign regiments which, after Waterloo, were formed into the Légion de Hohenlohe. In 1830, however, the corps was disbanded, but many of its former members rejoined in 1831, when the Légion Etrangère was raised.

Several new bodies of French troops, apart from the native regiments, came into being as a result of the conquest of Algeria, in particular the mounted Chasseurs d'Afrique, and the Zouaves, originally Arab infantry, but eventually entirely European in composition.

## The Mexican War (1846–48)

Texas, originally part of the republic of Mexico, was annexed by the United States on December 22, 1845, causing an immediate retaliation by Mexico. The invading United States Army did not have an easy time, however. The Mexicans were stubborn fighters, and the heroic resistance of the cadets at Chapultepec has become one of the minor epics of modern warfare.

The Mexican Army, now regularly organized, was dressed in a uniform modelled mostly on the French, the shako being almost a replica of the French pattern.

The cavalry branch included several regiments of lancers in different uniforms, such as the Activa Regiment in green, with red epaulettes, and the Guadalajara Regiment in dark blue, with red 'wings'. The Californian Lancers were more picturesque in their typically Mexican dress consisting of a black sombrero and a green, red or brown double-breasted shirt-jacket with silver buttons and white piping. Around the waist they wore a red sash, and their trousers were the Mexican bell-bot-

A United States dragoon.

54

tomed overalls which could be blue, brown or black. Evidently, there was little attempt to adhere to dress regulations.

The artillery was dressed as the infantry, except for red trousers in place of blue. These were worn over white gaiters. The officers' epaulettes were gold, on the French pattern.

On the United States side, the troops of General Zachary Taylor were clothed in a campaign dress of sober design. The coat was the fatigue jacket of 1833, which carried yellow facings for the cavalry—a color, incidentally, which some countries retained for that branch until 1945. In the United states, however, the yellow band on the forage cap, at this period, was unauthorized.

## The 1848 Revolutions in Europe

In the early months of 1848 France was in a ferment over the country's franchise. Louis-Philippe 'King of the French by the Grace of God and the Will of the People', had attempted to establish a constitutional monarchy on the British pattern. But the solid basis of a sound tradition was lacking and malcontents at each end of the social scale were quick to criticize shortcomings while ignoring the good points: the 1830 barricades were, after all, still a vivid memory.

On February 24, 1848, the industrial population of the Paris *faubourgs* stormed into the city, and the luckless Louis-Philippe was forced to flee to Great Britain.

The spirit of revolt quickly spread to other countries, the vast and heterogeneous Austrian Empire being a predestined victim. Riots broke out in Vienna, and Metternich escaped on March 13 to commiserate with Louis-Philippe in England.

The Austro-Hungarian Army at this time still wore the white short-tailed jacket, but the headdress was now a cylindrical shako. Regimental distinctions continued to be

Austrian infantry private.

shown by the color of the collar, cuffs and turnbacks combined with the white metal or brass of the buttons.

One of the most interesting revolts, however, occurred on March 1, 1848 at Neuchâtel. That territory—which, incidentally, had produced de Meuron's Regiment for the Dutch and British services, as well as Berthier's yellow-coated battalion for Napoleon —had been ceded to Prussia after the Napoleonic wars, and many of the 'Canaries' joined the newly formed Prussian Gardeschütze-Bataillon for service in Berlin. Fortunately for them, because they were then spared the agonizing duty of having to fire on their own countrymen when the latter marched down from the Jura Mountains to attack the castle at Neuchâtel. The Prussians were soon overcome, the inevitable republic proclaimed, and Neuchâtel became a Swiss canton.

The Prussian troops had now taken the famous spiked helmet into wear—but in a much taller version than the familiar 1914 pattern. The tunic was beginning to replace the long-skirted coat, and long trousers were being worn in preference to breeches and gaiters.

Private, British 4th Light Dragoons, 1854, and (*opposite*) British officers, 1854: 19th Foot and Royal Artillery.

## The Crimean War (1854–56)

The British Army was now wearing a close-fitting long-skirted coat and a tall cylindrical headdress with peaks in the front and back, reputedly introduced by the Prince Consort and known as the 'Albert' shako. Curiously enough, though, the whole style of dress was altered during the campaign, so that the troops who had set out in coats and shakos came back in tunics and kepis of French inspiration. In the artillery the change was even more spectacular, because here the shako was replaced by a fur busby with a scarlet bag and white hackle.

The Light Brigade of the British cavalry has been immortalized by the poet Tennyson; but while the epic charge of Balaclava was a magnificent piece of devotion and discipline, it contributed little if anything to the eventual outcome. '*C'est beau, mais ce n'est pas la guerre*', said a senior French officer — and indeed the less-publicized charge of the Heavy Brigade was actually more effective.

58

The Light Brigade consisted of the 4th and 13th Light
Dragoons, the 8th and 11th Hussars, and the 17th Lancers; the
Heavies were the 1st Royal Dragoons, the Scots Greys, the
Inniskillings and the 4th and 5th Dragoons. The Dragoon
Guards and Dragoons wore almost identical uniforms: red
coat and dark blue breeches, with a helmet of 'Roman' design;
the Scots Greys retained their traditional bearskin.

In the infantry, the more ample tunic appears to have been
adopted fairly early in the campaign. A photograph of Lieutenant W. G. D. Massy of the 19th Foot (The Green Howards)
shows him wearing a double-breasted tunic, which in the early
stages may well have been worn with the Albert shako. This
officer displayed extraordinary bravery at the storming of the
Redan, and was promoted captain in the field.

The French made good use of their Algerian troops in the
form of the Chasseurs d'Afrique and Zouaves. Of the former,
there were now four regiments, the 4th Regiment being

present at Balaclava and coming to the assistance of the sorely pressed British cavalry.

The Zouaves had originated as a native corps of Kabyles of the Zouaoua Tribe. By the time of the Crimean War, however, the Arab element had been transferred to the essentially native troops and the Zouaves remained an entirely European body, but still clad in Eastern style.

The 1st and 2nd Zouaves were in the Crimea, the regiments being distinguished by the color within the oval ornaments of their jackets: red for the 1st, white for the 2nd. The 3rd Regiment had primrose. A further distinction lay in the method of wearing the cap or *chéchia*: the 1st included it well over the right ear, the 2nd over the left. The Zouaves of the Guard were dressed in much the same manner, save that a white turban encircled the *chéchia*.

French troops, 1854. Trooper, 4th Chasseurs d'Afrique and infantry officer.

At this time the French Army boasted a fine force of cavalry of all arms—cuirassiers in blue, dragoons in green, hussars in various colors, chasseurs in green and lancers in blue—all with the universal red breeches.

The artillery wore the conventional all-blue with red facings—with a busby for the Guard and a shako for the line regiments.

Rank badges for officers were shown by the epaulettes. A captain wore two gold epaulettes with fringes; a lieutenant one on the left shoulder and another without fringe on the right, while a *sous-lieutenant* wore the same but on reverse shoulders. Field officers and generals wore gold epaulettes with a bullion fringe.

Non-commissioned officers were distinguished by the diagonal stripes above the cuffs, which were already in use under the *Ancien Régime*: one gold or silver for a sergeant, two red for a corporal and one for a 1st Class soldier or lance-corporal. A sergeant-major had two gold or silver stripes; and where the cuffs were pointed, all these stripes took the form of chevrons to conform with the shape of the cuff.

Private, French 2nd Zouaves, 1854.

Little contemporary evidence seems to exist on the dress of the Turkish Army at this time. This is unfortunate, since the Crimean War developed from the age-old quarrel between Russia and Turkey. Turkey, after some sporadic fighting on the frontiers, declared war on Russia in October 1853, with the result that the Turkish Fleet was destroyed at Sinope on November 30 of the same year.

This defeat alarmed Britain and France, fearing a strong and confident Russia might threaten Europe, and the two countries, joined later by Sardinia, declared war on the Tsar.

Meanwhile, the Turks had won several actions in succession, but the Russians retaliated with a determined offensive, penetrating deep into the Balkan Peninsula. Perhaps a little too deep, for the lines of communication became somewhat stretched—and in the north an Austrian army of observation was poised. The Russians withdrew.

Yet Russia's power at sea was still a formidable menace, and there was no longer a Turkish fleet to hold it in check. Consequently, Great Britain and France were determined to strike at the naval base of Sebastopol in the Crimea, and on September 7, 1854 a convoy of 150 ships crossed the Black Sea.

A well-known photograph by Roger Fenton shows the British, French and Turkish commanders in conference, in which the Pasha wears a dark coat, with presumably gold lace, and a fez, probably red. A contemporary print of the Royal Welsh Fusiliers shows, in the background, a Turkish officer in blue, with a red fez, in conversation with two British officers.

Of the other ranks we know little, although Knoetel informs us (*Handbuch der Uniformkunde*) that the infantry wore a short blue jacket with an upright red collar, blue trousers and red fez, while the cavalry was dressed in a dark blue tunic with hussar braiding and three rows of buttons. A gray cloak, with hood, was issued to all arms.

The uniforms of the Sardinian Army at this period formed the basis of the pattern adopted later in the forces of the new Kingdom of Italy. The cavalry consisted of six regiments of heavy cavalry in blue tunics and blue-gray overalls with bands in the facing color, while the helmet was a handsome affair of classical design with an imposing brass comb and the White Cross of Savoy on the front. There was also one regi-

(*Left*) Turkish officer, 1855;
(*right*) trooper, Sardinian Genoa
Cavalry Regiment, 1855.

ment of light cavalry clothed much the same as the heavies, except for a shako and facings in light blue.

The Russians, for their part, had recognized for centuries that winter was one of their best allies. That the terrible weather in the Crimea proved a valuable asset to the Russians cannot be doubted, although they too must have suffered considerably from its effects.

The full dress of the Russian Army, always spectacular and colorful, naturally enough was not worn in the field, and the fighting dress of the Tsar's soldiers consisted normally of the black leather helmet with its tall flame-shaped spike, and a long greatcoat of heavy drab cloth.

The Russian cavalry, apart from the complex formations of Cossacks, consisted of cuirassiers, dragoons, hussars and lancers: all in particularly splendid attire, especially in the

Russian Privates, 1854. (*Left*)
31st Infantry Regiment, and
(*right*) artillery of the Guard.

Gunner, Russian horse artillery of the Guard, 1855.

Guard. The Horse Grenadiers of the Guard deserve especial notice for their remarkable helmet, conventional in its main part, but crowned by a black fur crest which was set, not back and front in the usual way, but crosswise, from temple to temple over the top. It was further decorated at the back by a hanging bag of red edged in yellow lace. The drummers' crests were red, and they wore a profusion of yellow, or gold, chevrons on each sleeve, and laced swallows'-nests under their red epaulettes. Their most remarkable feature was that they carried infantry-pattern side-drums.

The artillery, the men who served the guns at Balaclava, must have worn infantry-style uniform and, probably, dark green flat caps with a black band and red piping. In full dress they would have a dark green uniform with black facings and red piping, while the helmet would be of the general-service pattern. A specimen of this headdress is preserved in the Castle Museum at York, and it displays no other ornaments than crossed guns in brass and a somewhat unlikely white-over-crimson plume issuing from a brass socket in lieu of spike.

## Headdresses

Up to the end of the eighteenth century headwear was usually no more than an adaptation of the civilian tricorne, although helmets of various forms were often worn in the cavalry. With the elaboration of military dress, however, more distinctive designs began to emerge, frequently of a national character; these, incidentally, were often copied by other armies.

Thus the French kepi reappeared in Denmark, the United States, Russia and numerous South American republics, to name but a few. The spiked helmet, probably of Eastern origin,

F

H

was worn in Russia, Great Britain, Spain, Portugal and Germany. The hussar busby was based on the national fur cap of Hungary.

The illustrations on these pages show: (a) Austro-Hungarian grenadier cap, early nineteenth century; (b) Austro-Hungarian helmet; (c) British 'Belgic' cap, 1812–16; (d) French busby, First Empire; (e) Russian dragoon helmet, 1900–14; (f) Norwegian guardsman's hat, 1900–14; (g) French kepi, 1900–14; (h) Swiss shako, 1900–14; (i) Bavarian officer's helmet, 1914; (j) French helmet, 1916; (k) German helmet, 1917.

I

J

K

## The Indian Mutiny (1858)

Great Britain had hardly recovered from the Crimean War when trouble broke out in India. There had been several outbreaks there as early as 1764, and discontent was present in some form for a long time. However, in July 1856 a general enlistment order, resulting from the war in Persia, aroused Hindu fears that they might lose caste if they had to cross the sea.

Further, the rumors of British reverses in the Crimea gave cause for disquiet, so that what with the prophecy of British rule ending a hundred years after Plassey (1757) and sundry minor disturbances, the atmosphere was truly ripe for agitators, who promptly exploited the fact that the cartridges for the new Minie rifle were greased with the fat of cows and pigs. To listen to them, this was obviously an attempt to force the sepoys into Christianity when they bit the greased cartridges and thus became outcasts from their own religions. At Berhampur, on February 27, 1858, the 19th Bengal Infantry Regiment refused

Officer, Hodson's Horse, 1857, in white service uniform

Private and sergeant-major, British infantry, 1857

to parade to draw percussion caps — and even the old-pattern cartridges were rejected.

On April 24 eighty-five men of the native cavalry at Meerut refused their cartridges and were promptly jailed. On the following day, however, while the British troops were at church parade, the remainder of the native regiments took up their arms and released their imprisoned comrades. The hysteria spread rapidly, and two native infantry regiments shot their officers. The revolt had now reached dangerous proportions.

A number of irregular units existed in India at the time of the Mutiny. Hodson's Horse was famous among them: a corps

Sepoy, 20th Bombay Native
Regiment, 1857

which was an amalgamation of several independent units in the Punjab, embodied under Lieutenant W. S. R. Hodson in 1857.

European officers and other ranks often wore white or light khaki uniforms, the latter probably being the white outfit dyed. The head-dress in this case was usually the undress cap encased in a white or khaki cap-cover with a neck-curtain at the back. A painting done at Subzimandi, Delhi, in 1857 shows two European soldiers in a light khaki kit bearing a remarkable resemblance to present-day battledress. The unit is not indicated, but the grenade on the belt-plates would suggest the 2nd Fusiliers, who were certainly present.

Unlike the French in Algeria, the British had made little attempt to design uniforms in keeping with native dress. Admittedly, the head-dress was always based on the native pattern, but for the rest of the uniform it was simply a matter of providing British regulation coats with the appropriate facings and lace. At this period even the trousers were the dark infantry pattern, or white for the very hot weather. Boots, however, were distinctly unpopular, and the startling spectacle of a soldier in sandals, or even barefoot, was a common sight.

In the cavalry it was a different matter. Breeches and boots were a necessity; but on the other hand, many units wore the native *kurta,* or smock-like tunic.

As time went on, the rebels entrenched themselves solidly in Dehli, which was accordingly besieged by the British. Hodson's Horse was present with the attackers, in khaki uniforms with red facings. The word 'khaki' is derived from the Persian, meaning dust or ashes; it is interesting to note that the official name for the color was 'drab'.

The Gurkhas, that unique body of Himalayan mountaineers, were first taken into the service of the Honorable East India Company in 1815, not as Indian troops, but as subjects of the King of Nepal and allies of the British.

Being wiry and active, the Gurkhas were formed into rifle regiments and dressed as such in dark green with sundry minor distinctions of a regimental character. They remained faithful to the British during the Mutiny and

Rifleman, 2nd Gurkhas, 1857

71

performed many deeds of valor, often making good use of their national weapon, the *kukri*, that cross between sword and knife that could intimidate the bravest enemy. The Gurkhas' motto reads, 'It is better to die than to live a coward', and these tough little soldiers have never failed their watchword.

The Punjab Irregular Force (P.I.F.) came into being when a number of independent units, working on the frontier between the Punjab and Wazirabad, were brought under a single command in the early part of the nineteenth century. The 'Piffers' mounted branch comprised the Corps of Guides, raised in December 1846, and five regiments of cavalry.

The 1st Regiment was formed at Peshawar in 1849 and clothed in native dress, 'with the sole addition', according to the 'Illustrated London News' of 1857, 'of the long boots of European horsemen' (Carman). The British officers wore a dark blue jacket with a buff collar and pointed cuffs in the same color. There was silver lace tracing around the collar, and the cuffs had a silver crow's foot. Silver lace was set all around the garment, which carried silver plaited cords on the shoulders. The Regiment later became Prince Albert Victor's Own Cavalry.

Sowar, 2nd Punjab
Cavalry, 1857.

Express Camel trooper, 6th Irregular Cavalry, 1850, and sowar, 1st Punjab Cavalry, c. 1857.

The 2nd Punjab Cavalry—later 22nd Sam Browne's Cavalry—was raised at Lahore in April 1849. Sam Browne was second-in-command when it was formed, and he was no more than a lieutenant at the time. He soon acquired fame, though, in some fierce hand-to-hand fighting in which he lost one arm from a sword-cut at the shoulder; yet his far better known, though less spectacular, achievement was his 'invention' of the cross-belt for officers which bears his name and is still worn.

Bengal, too, had its own regiments of irregular cavalry, some of which comprised a detachment of camel troops, such as the 6th. This regiment was raised in 1838 for service with the King of Oudh, under the name of The Cavalry Regiment of the Oudh Auxiliary Force. When it was absorbed in the Bengal Army in 1840, it received the title of 6th Regiment of Bengal Irregular Cavalry.

In 1848, the European officers of the regiment wore a black helmet with a white falling plume—a close imitation of the Prussian pickelhaube of the period, reputed to have been given to the regiment, as an honor, by the King of Prussia after Prince Waldemar's visit to Sind.

73

## The Franco-Austrian War in Italy (1858–59)

First class gunner, French artillery of the Guard

*'L'Empire, c'est la paix'*. Thus the Emperor Napoleon III to a sceptical world in need of reassurance: a world, indeed, that had found little opportunity to observe that 'Empire' did indeed mean 'Peace'. Nor could it derive much comfort from the spectacle of that monarch setting himself up as a champion of the liberty of nations.

Italy was one of his particular protegées, and Garibaldi's march on Rome provided a ready incentive. Austria saw it in a different light, as well she might, with many of her possessions threatened; nor were the French Catholics impressed, since they feared the downfall of the Papacy. Things came to a head in 1858 when the Emperor just missed being assassinated by an Italian patriot, Orsini, whereupon he decided that he really must 'do something for Italy'.

France and Austria were soon at each other's throats, with Piedmont-Sardinia on the French side. In the French Army, this period is perhaps its most colorful in the matter of dress, reflecting the scintillating light-heartedness of an era that could produce Offen-

'Cantinière', French lancers of the Guard

bach's *'Daughter of the Drum Major'* and, incidentally, the early numbers of *'La Vie Parisienne'*. Who, for instance, can resist the charm of the delightful little *cantinières* in their gay uniforms? The time had come when those dedicated persons were no longer mere camp-followers picking up and wearing odd items of discarded clothing. They now had a regulation uniform of their own, and if the contemporary prints err on the side of glamour, even the fat and *forte* among them could hardly fail to benefit from the change.

The French Imperial Guard was more resplendent than ever, as if the nephew of Napoleon I was bent on outdoing his uncle. There were lancers in dazzling white blending with light blue and scarlet; guides and chasseurs in green and gold; dragoons and cuirassiers in shining brass and steel.

The artillery was perhaps the most soberly dressed of all this spendid company, in dark blue and red, with a busby for the Guard and a shako for the line.

The French infantry units had hardly changed since the Crimean War which, after all, had ended only four years earlier, but on the Austrian

Hungarian infantry private

side much had occurred since we last discussed that army. True, the white coat had remained, but it was now a double-breasted tunic, introduced in 1849, with the regiment indicated by the color of the collar, cuffs, shoulder-straps and piping, as well as by the metal of the buttons. In service dress the tunic was plain, with the regimental color shown on the collar-patch but nowhere else.

As before, the Hungarian regiments wore mid-blue close-fitting trousers with short ankle-boots, while the shako had become a slightly conical affair, smaller at the top than it was at the bottom.

The jäger, or light infantry, had originated as early as the Seven Years War and were now clothed in a gray-green uniform, officially described as 'pike-gray' with green facings.

In the cavalry, the cuirassiers and dragoons had now adopted the white tunic and dispensed with the crest on their helmets, while light blue overalls were taken into wear in 1840. Hussars wore uniforms of light or dark blue, according to the regi-

Austrian Kaiserjäger officer

ment, with a further distinction in the color of the shako, which could be green, white or scarlet. The lancers were in dark green, with the regimental color shown on the lance-cap; and the artillery wore the traditional brown tunic with red facings.

The two most outstanding battles of this war were perhaps Magenta on June 4, 1859 and Solferino on June 24, 1859. The latter was marked by much desperate fighting, the Austrians losing some 22,000 men and the Franco-Sardinians, 17,000. It was witnessed by a citizen of Geneva, Henri Dunant, who was so appalled by the sufferings of the wounded, that, on his return, he collected a few friends and with their assistance founded that institution which has since developed into the International Red Cross.

However, the war was drawing to its close. Prussia, ever watchful, was threatening intervention, and an armistice was signed by Napoleon III and Francis Joseph of Austria at Villefranche on July 11 of the same year.

## The War of the Danish Duchies (1864)

It is the unfortunate destiny of frontier provinces to be in constant dispute between their neighbors: the unwilling, though often resigned victims of interstate tugs-of-war, sometimes going to one country, sometimes to another.

Schleswig and Holstein were two small provinces lying between Prussia and Denmark. Half of the people spoke German; the other half spoke Danish. They had been ruled by the Danish king since 1813 but were not formally part of that country. In 1863 Denmark annexed these two provinces outright.

On February 18, 1864, some Prussian hussars on patrol

(*Left*) officer, Austrian 27th Infantry Regiment; (*right*) officer, Prussian dragoons of the Guard.

crossed the border and occupied the Danish village of Kolding. Denmark complained, and Bismarck, plainly seeking annexation, replied as might be expected, prevailing on Austria to support his case.

The Prussians and Austrians attacked; and the Danes, though outnumbered, put up a stubborn resistance. In two weeks, however, Denmark was defeated.

The Austrian infantry had now given up its tall cylindrical shako in favor of a conical variety not unlike the French kepi. In the field, this was encased in an oilskin cover.

In the cavalry, which consisted of cuirassiers, dragoons, hussars and lancers, there had been little change since the war in Italy. The cuirassiers discarded their cuirass in 1860, and the dragoons, who were now wearing a modernized version of the classical helmet, had absorbed the chevaulegers in 1852. The hussars, twelve regiments strong, were clothed in light or

Trooper, Austrian 2nd Dragoons

Warrant officer, 4th Magdeburg Field Artillery Regiment.

dark blue jackets, and had breeches and pelisses to match. Their shakos were of different colors according to their regiments.

The lancers were still in dark green with red facings, and had reverted to the yellow epaulettes which had been discarded about 1840.

In the Prussian Army, the pickelhaube was now firmly established as the standard headdress, although in the artillery the spike was replaced by a ball.

The Prussian dragoons at this time were wearing a light blue tunic, a color which was theirs since Napoleonic times, with facings in regimental colorings. The cuirassiers were in white and the hussars, as usual, in uniforms of different colors for every regiment. A black busby had been in wear since 1850 and the pelisse was discontinued in 1853.

The lancers, or uhlans, wore the traditional lancers' dress of Polish origin (i.e., the square-topped lance-cap and distinctive tunic, or *ulanka,* of blue cloth with regimental facing colors).

In the infantry of the line, a dark blue tunic had been authorized in 1843, with red collar-patches. The trousers

Danish troops; guide and infantry private.

were of a very dark blue, almost black, with red piping down the sides.

The light infantry were termed *jäger* and wore the 1843 tunic, but in dark green with red collar-patches. A helmet was issued originally, but replaced in 1854 by a tall conical shako with a peak back and front.

The Danish infantry was in dark blue kepis and tunics, piped red, and light blue trousers, while the dragoons and hussars wore light blue tunics with a 'Roman' helmet for the dragoons and probably a shako for the hussars.

Peace was signed on August 1, 1864 and ratified on October 30. The King of Denmark renounced all his rights in favor of the Emperor of Austria and the King of Prussia. The duchies were merged in the larger question of the relations between these two powers, who were soon fighting each other; Prussia finally established her supremacy at Sadowa in 1866.

### The American Civil War (1861–65)

To say that the war arose from the rival attitudes of the North and South to the question of slavery is to understate the case. Admittedly, this was no doubt the primary matter in dispute, but the root cause was more likely to have been the profound differences of character in the Northern and Southern citizens of the United States. The Northerners were eager and businesslike, often the descendants of men who, dissatisfied with their lot, had left Europe to seek a new life in America; while the Southerner, heir to an old tradition of colonial prosperity, was more easy-going and self-assured. His America was almost entirely agricultural, while the North was expanding industrially and commercially.

The trouble started when eleven Southern states decided to secede from the Union. This was in early 1861, and the seceding states, calling themselves the Confederate states of America, were Virginia,. North and South Carolina, Georgia, Florida, Alabama, Mississippi, Louisiana, Texas, Arkansas and Tennessee. In Missouri, Kentucky and Maryland opinion was divided, but these states eventually sided with the North.

Jefferson Davis was elected President of the Confederacy as the government prepared to meet an attack by the Union. The Southern states had earlier ceded land to the Federal Government for the purpose of coast defense. They now considered themselves entitled to resume occupation of the forts, and finding diplomatic approaches ineffectual, decided to adopt sterner measures. Accordingly, Fort Sumter, at Charleston, was bombarded by the South Carolinians on April 12, 1861. The Northern garrison held out as long as possible, then surrendered, to be conveyed by Southern warships to Union territory.

In spite of this generous gesture, however, the affront

Three of the uniforms worn by the Federal forces in the Civil War. (*Above*) Engineer officer. (*Opposite, left*) a private of the 5th New York Zouaves, one of the many zouave units whose uniforms copied the French model almost exactly. The uniform (*opposite, right*) is a cavalry officer's.

remained. Besides, lives had been lost, and President Lincoln called out 75,000 troops. A few states refused their contifigents, but a large number of men volunteered from civilian life: many more, in fact, than had been requested.

In addition, there were numbers of volunteer units already in existence, wearing all manner of dress. Uniforms of French design were very popular, and the quantity of 'zouave' regiments which sprang up, based on the French, on both sides, was truly astounding. In the regular army, the French influence was marked especially by the kepi which was worn in practically all branches—an almost exact replica of the cap then issued to the French troops.

The Confederates, for their part, started organizing their army on a proper footing. Dress regulations were promulgated, setting out a uniform consisting of a gray tunic and light blue trousers. The kepi had a dark blue band around the base and the top was made in the particular color of the branch concerned: yellow for the čavalry, red for the artillery and light blue for the infantry. These colors were repeated in the collar, cuffs and piping on the tunic, which was double-breasted and had brass buttons.

Badges of rank consisted of short horizontal gold bars on the collar and stars for field officers, supplemented by large Austrian knots, after the French pattern, in gold tracing on the sleeves. The cuffs were pointed, and there were no ornaments on the shoulders. However, considering that the Government had a war on its hands, it is unlikely that the regulation uniform was ever worn to any great extent.

On the other hand, records exist of some really magnificent uniforms in this hurriedly assembled army, such as the one worn by the drum major of the 1st Virginia Regiment.

If, as is probable, the volunteer units on both sides were allowed to design their own outfits, then it is not surprising to find the most unaccountable vagaries of dress. The period was still one in which the soldier went blithely to war, although in this bitter conflict—the first of the wars fought with modern techniques—he returned much sobered. True, the bandsmen in all ages and all countries were always dressed in a more spectacular manner than the rank-and-file, a principle which was acknowledged even in the more

Troops of the Confederate Army.
(*Left*) drum major of the 1st
Virginia Regiment, and (*right*)
gunner, 1st Tennessee Artillery.

85

Federal bandsman

somber clothing of the Northern regular forces.

Originally both Northern and Southern troops were volunteers, but as the struggle continued it became necessary to resort to conscription, first in the Confederacy and then in the Union. Even so, the South was by far the weaker contestant, both numerically and otherwise, and could seldom oppose equal numbers to the Northern troops in the field.

The zouave units were picturesque in the extreme, especially in view of the flights of sartorial fancy which their costume invited. Many copied the French model almost literally, such as the Ellsworth Zouaves and the 5th New York, who both wore blue jackets and scarlet breeches. Hawkin's New York Zouaves were in dark blue with purple facings, while the Wallace Zouaves of Illinois favored light blue. Berdan's Sharpshooters were dressed entirely in grass green, and the Massachusetts Iron Brigade was in light blue with black felt hats.

The most remarkable regiment was surely the 79th Cameron Highlanders, a body of Scottish volunteers who had borrowed not only the British regiment's title, but its number as well. Understandably, they could not call themselves 'The Queen's Own', but they wore Highland dress, with a Cameron of Erracht kilt—and they conformed to the French trend of the times with a pair of fringed epaulettes. The regiment had been formed in 1859 in New York under the command of Colonel James Cameron, a brother of Abraham Lincoln's Secretary of War, and in May 1861, at a strength of 895 men, it marched down Broadway on its way to the war. Two months later it distinguished itself at the first Battle of Bull Run, at which Colonel Cameron was killed. This was the first major battle of the war, and like the second Battle of Bull Run, in August 1862, was won by the Confederates.

This was in the early stages, but as the war dragged on and each side became increasingly bitter, as only civil war antagonists can, a deep determination gradually took the place of the initial enthusiasm. The two armies showed equal resolution in battle, although their discipline was somewhat elastic by European standards. Yet, this did not prevent individual acts of

Federal infantry sergeant

Uniforms of the Confederate Army. (*Left*) the Virginia cavalry. (*Opposite page*) a private of the Louisiana Tigers, a zouave regiment, and a sergeant, the Mississippi Rifles.

gallantry on both sides—indeed, it may have favored them.

Irish brigades were present in both Northern and Southern armies, with the tragic result that in some battles, such as Fredericksburg, for example, they shot each other down regardless of kinship.

In the Southern states, the popularity of the zouaves can more readily be explained from the large number of French-speaking inhabitants of these former French colonies. In fact, the dress of the Louisiana Zouaves, as opposed to Louisiana Tigers, was, except for small details, an exact replica of the French uniform.

As in most other armies, the metal buttons of the tunics were used as an additional means of identification. In the Confederacy, a general's buttons carried the badge of an eagle surrounded by a circle of stars. The cavalry had a letter 'C', the artillery a letter 'A', and the infantry's showed the number of the unit.

In the Union, the arm-of-service designation was shown on the cap or the hat, the cavalry wearing crossed swords,

tne artillery crossed guns with a numeral above, and the infantry a bugle-horn of conventional design, with the unit's number displayed within the circle of the horn. Rifle regiments had a bugle of modern pattern, placed vertically with the bell downward, and the numeral inside the loop of the instrument. General officers wore the initials 'U.S.' in Gothic capitals within an open wreath of laurels.

The war ended with the victory of the Army of the Potomac and the surrender of General Robert E. Lee, commander-in-chief of the Confederate armies, at Appomattox Court House, on April 9, 1865. The President of the United States proclaimed a general amnesty on May 29, 1865; but there was no rejoicing, and no hard conditions. Slavery was now abolished throughout the United States of America, and a period of great social and economic changes began. The Confederates surrendered their equipment and pledged never again to take up arms against the Federal Union.

## The Franco-German War (1870–71)

After Prussia's decisive victory over Austria at Sadowa in 1866, it became abundantly clear that Bismarck's ambitions would not stay at that. Napoleon III, successful in other wars, was a potential menace: an armed conflict, therefore, became inevitable.

France, on her side, had little cause for anxiety. The Chassepot breech-loading rifle, which was now being issued, was far superior to the German needle-gun, and the new *mitrailleuse* was a recently invented and deadly machine-gun. Unfortunately, time was short and there was delay in equipping all units of the army with the new weapons. Therefore, in order to gain time, the Emperor sent General Lebrun to Vienna with a view to enlisting Austrian support; and Italy was also approached.

The plan was for the French armies to concentrate in Northern Bavaria, to be joined there by the Austrians and Italians, and then for all to press on to Berlin. However, the prospect of revenge did not appeal to the Austrians, and Italy remained lukewarm. Nor was Bavaria, so often a faithful ally of Franch, dis-

French military uniforms of the 1870's. (*Above*) an officer of the Garde Mobile, a reserve body consisting mainly of infantry. (*Opposite*) a naval rating and an Algerian 'tirailleur'.

posed to court further trouble with Prussia, after having
resolutely opposed her in the Danish question and actively
sided with Austria in 1866. Napoleon decided to act alone.

The French Army had plenty of experience of warfare and
could face the coming events with confidence. In composition and dress it remained practially unchanged as, in that
fateful August of 1870, it went out to meet the German divisions that had crossed the frontier in Lorraine and Alsace.

The infantry of the line was wearing the field service
order which it retained until 1914: the red kepi, blue greatcoat turned back at the sides and the traditional red trousers.

Corporal, French cuirassiers of the Guard.

In 1870, however, red epaulettes were also worn.

The light infantry—the chasseurs à pied—disdained the greatcoat and fought in their dark blue tunics and blue-gray trousers, with green epaulettes on their shoulders.

As the war went on, with several reverses for the French, the reserves were called out to fill the gaps. In this category, the Garde Mobile proved a valuable asset in the French defense: a body consisting mainly of infantry, clothed in the style of the times, but in light blue trousers with a broad scarlet band. The kepi was in reversed colors and there were no epaulettes. The artillery units wore practically the same uniform as the regular gunners.

Colonial troops and even the Navy were called in, as every effort was made to increase the numerical strength, and the Zouaves, Chasseurs d'Afrique and Tirailleurs Algériens did particularly well, to say nothing of those picturesque Arab horsemen, the Spahis. The Tirailleurs distinguished themselves in a memorable action at Wissembourg, in Alsace, where a memorial still stands as a tribute to their gallantry.

The French Navy, naturally enough, wore conventional naval dress, and could be recognized by the characteristic red ball-tuft on the top of the cap and the white chinstrap which was usually worn over the top.

The cuirassiers of the Guard differed from the line chiefly in the matter of epaulettes, which were white in the Guard and red for the others. In full dress they also wore white aiguillettes at the right shoulder.

In the early part of the war, many regiments of chasseurs à cheval were still wearing the green, black-braided jacket of hussar pattern. The busby carried a red-over-green plume

Trooper, French 4th Chasseurs à Cheval.

in front, and the red overalls had a double band of dark green. However, a new uniform had been designed early in 1870, and some regiments turned out in a blue tunic, laced hussar-fashion with five black 'ribs', while the overall-stripes now became blue. The plumes were laid aside for active service.

The dragoons and lancers, too, changed their style of dress: the dragoons from green to blue, and the lancers discarded the coat with its colored plastron in favor of a plain blue tunic.

This conflict is often called the Franco-Prussian War, but although Prussia was without a doubt the prime mover, the other German states were also fully involved. Bavaria and Saxony, Baden and Württemberg, all threw in their lot with the powerful Prussia.

In many respects, the German uniforms were similar from country to country, especially in the infantry, although the pickelhaube was not introduced in Bavaria until after the campaign. Where the helmet was in wear, each state had a different helmet-plate to distinguish it from the others; thus,

Trumpeter, Prussian 11th Uhlans

A private of the Bavarian infantry and an officer of the Saxon infantry.

Prussia used the eagle; Württemberg, the royal coat-of arms; Baden, the griffin; and Saxony, the star. The general pattern, however, closely followed the Prussian model: dark blue tunics and almost black trousers, except in Bavaria where the blue was lighter. In marching order the ends of the trousers were tucked into the boots.

German bandsmen, trumpeters and drummers were distinguished from their comrades by a pair of 'swallows'-nests' on the shoulders. These were usually in the facing color and covered with bars of gold or silver lace placed vertically in the infantry and diagonally in the cavalry.

The Bavarian infantry retained its own pattern of helmet, with the black fur crest in place of the spike. The shape of the helmet was much like the Prussian, but in this case the badge on the front took the form of a crowned cypher 'L' in brass or white metal. The ammunition-pouches were still worn suspended from the waistbelt, and the system of wearing

Prussian Cuirassier trooper

the greatcoat rolled bandolier-fashion was much in favor.

It seems a little ironical that, a bare sixty years earlier, troops from Baden had been fighting for Napoleon in the Peninsular. However, France was no longer the power that it once was, and the Grand Duke foresaw a much better future on the Prussian side. This attitude was reflected quite definitely in the Prussian-style uniform worn by his troops, although he was careful to retain his own emblem in the helmet-plate.

The Prussian cuirassiers did not shrink from going to war in their white uniform, which must have suffered considerably in action; and their helmet was an interesting survival of the 'lobster' of the English Civil War period, with its long scaled neck-protector. The French helmet had the same in a smaller version but relied mainly on the horsehair streamer for protection from sword cuts.

In Bavaria, the crested helmet appeared again in the green-clad chevaulegers, and in Württemberg, somewhat surprisingly, the headdress was a form of kepi, which was worn both in the infantry and cavalry until 1870, when the cavalry went over to the spiked helmet.

The end of the war is well known: Bazaine's surrender at Metz, followed by the Emperor's defeat at Sedan in 1871; and finally the heroic but hopeless resistance of the new republican army and the long-drawn-out siege of Paris.

Germany exacted harsh terms, including the cession of the whole of Alsace and much of Lorraine to Prussia. France had no option but to comply and peace was signed in the Hall of Mirrors at Versailles. As a crowning humiliation, the King of Prussia was acclaimed Emperor of Germany on the same occasion.

Bismarck had won again. He could not himself propose William of Prussia for the Imperial throne, but the mentally unbalanced King of Bavaria did it for him.

A private of the Baden
nfantry.

## The Spanish-American War (1898)

By the end of the nineteenth century, Cuba was one of the last remaining Spanish possessions in America, and a cause of friction between Spain and the United States. In January 1898, the United States had called her warships home, and on February 15 the battleship *Maine* was destroyed by an explosion while lying in Havana harbor, with a loss of 266 lives. The cause was never clearly established, although the evidence seemed to point to a mine. On February 20 the United States demanded the withdrawal of Spain from Cuba and two days later blockaded the Cuban ports. Spain declared war on February 24.

It was mostly a sea war. United States troops landed unopposed on the Cuban beaches, but Spanish resistance stiffened as they progressed inland. At El Caney, in particular,

United States troops. A Rough Rider in field uniform, and (*right*) a light artillery officer.

United States artillery private in shirt sleeve order.

the garrison held out for a considerable time despite the great American supremacy in numbers.

Among the United States' troops were the 1st Volunteer Cavalry—the famous Rough Riders—commanded by Colonel Leonard Woodward, with Lieutenant Colonel Theodore Roosevelt as second-in-command. Roosevelt's attack on 700 Spaniards opposite San Juan Hill was later to become famous.

The Americans were being issued a khaki uniform for field service, with the flat-brimmed felt hat, but few of the troops sent to Cuba had acquired it before they sailed. Consequently, most of them were in the blue field uniform adopted in 1880. The Rough Riders, however, are usually shown in a blue shirt and khaki breeches with brown leather gaiters.

In the cavalry and infantry, full dress at this period bore some resemblance to the British, principally in the blue spiked helmet, which carried a falling plume in the arm-of-service color on ceremonial occasions. The helmet-plate was in the form of a brass American eagle.

The Medical Department was identified by a gilt cross on the collar, but on service a

Red Cross armband was also worn for easier recognition. Stretcher-bearers, not being qualified medical troops, did not wear the Red Cross armband, but a plain red band instead.

The war was not confined to Cuba. The Philippines were also in Spanish hands, and an American squadron eventually appeared outside Manila, which was beseiged for some time by Major General Wesley Merritt, with about 20,000 men, until the Spanish Captain-General, surrounded by insurgents, was obliged to surrender on May 13, 1898.

The Spanish tropical kit consisted of a white duck uniform with blue stripes, and a straw hat like the version worn by British sailors at the time. Infantry uniform for field service at home, however, was very similar to the French, with red trousers and a blue-gray turned-back greatcoat. Instead of epaulettes the Spaniards had red shoulder-pads in the form of 'wings'; and on the feet they wore their distinctive national footwear, lacing up the leg.

Gunner, Spanish artillery

Spanish troops. Infantry private and officer, Princesa Hussars.

The cavalry consisted of mounted *cazadores,* or light cavalry, lancers, and hussars. The *cazadores* wore a light blue hussar tunic with black braiding and white-metal buttons, embodying a red collar and pointed cuffs of the same color. Breeches were red with light blue bands, and the kepi was light blue with a red band at the top. The lancers wore the same uniform, except that they had a steel helmet with spike and other fittings in brass.

The Princesa's Hussars were dressed in light blue, with a white pelisse and kepi. The Pavia Hussars were similarly attired, except that in this regiment the tunic was red and the pelisse light blue. The kepi was of a darker shade of blue. In both regiments the braiding was yellow.

The Americans invaded Puerto Rico on July 21, 1898. It was occupied almost without resistance, and the population turned out to be very favorably disposed toward their new occupiers. When peace was signed on August 12, 1898, over three hundred years of Spanish rule in America came to an end.

Sergeant, 6th Inniskilling Dragoons, 1900.

## The South African War (1899–1902)

In the Orange Free State and Transvaal, the large number of British and other *Uitlanders* (immigrants) had tried, unsuccessfully, to obtain the franchise. By 1895 they formed a majority of the population, owned half the land and nine-tenths of the property—but had no say in the affairs of South Africa.

Obviously, this situation could not continue. A number of suggestions were made, without result. A ten-point memorandum was prepared, setting out the Uitlanders' grievances, but still Boer President Paul Kruger remained adamant. Finally, in desperation, Englishman Dr. Jameson set out on his abortive raid on December 29, 1895. The idea was to stir up rebellion in Pretoria, but when the 500 partisans arrived, the town was full of Boers. Dr. Jameson had been warned, but he refused to listen and was arrested on January 2, 1896.

The German Emperor then took the unheard-of step of sending a telegram to President Kruger congratulating him on repelling the raiders 'without appealing for the help of a friendly power'. The British Government reminded his Imperial Majesty in reply that the London Convention reserved the supervising of the Transvaal's foreign affairs to Great Britain alone.

Naturally, however, all this did not make the situation any better, and things finally came to a head when war was declared on October 11, 1899 in response to an ultimatum from the Transvaal.

British troops began to arrive in Cape Town soon afterward, dressed entirely in khaki and wearing the Wolseley type of pith helmet. In this uniform there was little to distinguish one regiment from another, but on dress occasions, at home, there was still plenty of color.

The cavalry, except for the Royal Horse Guards, hussars and lancers, were in scarlet tunics, with helmets for the Life Guards, Dragoon Guards and Dragoons, and bearskin caps for the Royal Scots Greys, as before. The others remained in blue.

The infantry of the line, also in scarlet, was now wearing the dark blue helmet, with a brass spike and star-shaped

British infantry, 1900. Private, the Highland Light Infantry (*top*) and sergeant, the Rifle Brigade.

plate bearing the regimental badge in the center. Fusiliers wore the racoon-skin cap, and the light infantry wore a dark green helmet, while the rifle regiments were in their traditional dark green, almost black, uniform with the small black fur cap. The Highland regiments were kilted in the appropriate tartan, except the Highland Light Infantry, who wore light infantry uniform with a diced border round the shako and trews of Mackenzie tartan.

The Royal Field Artillery, after experimenting with a spiked helmet, replaced the spike by a ball in August 1881. The helmet-plate was the regimental badge in the form of the Royal coat-of-arms above a field gun in profile, and the uniform remained dark blue with a scarlet collar. The Royal Horse Artillery retained the busby and yellow-braided jacket.

The Boer commandos, on the other hand, did not wear a uniform as such, the only concession to military appearance being a varying quantity of cartridge-belts.

However, uniforms were certainly designed for the artillery of the Transvaal and Orange Free State, and a photograph exists of an officer of the Transvaal artillery in a dark blue outfit and a kepi very much like the pattern worn in the Netherlands at the time. The rank was shown by means of stars on the collar, a major having three.

There was also what is described as a mouse-colored corduroy service dress which was worn with a slouch hat; but full dress consisted of a dark blue tunic, braided hussar-fashion, dark blue breeches and a white helmet of British design with a white falling plume.

The Orange Free State artillery were dressed in mouse-colored corduroy, like the Transvaalers, with either a slouch hat or an undress cap bearing the arms of the Republic as a badge. About 1880 there was a blue full-dress uniform with a helmet bearing a white-and-orange falling plume.

The War ended with the signing of the Treaty of Vereeniging on May 31, 1902. The Boers accepted British sovereignty, and Great Britain allowed a grant of £ 3,000,000 in compensation for the destruction of farms during the two and a half years of fighting.

British infantryman and Transvaal artillery officer.

## Cuffs, Epaulettes, Shoulder Straps, Loops and Wings

The early cuffs were designed to be lowered in bad weather to protect the hands; and the buttons (which later became mere ornaments) served originally to keep them in position when turned up. This continual buttoning and unbuttoning caused considerable wear on the buttonholes, which soon had to be strengthened by 'loops' of braid. These gradually appeared on cuffs and coats alike and in time served no more than a decorative purpose.

The origin of epaulettes is obscure. They started as very small ornaments in the eighteenth century and assumed ever-increasing proportions until by the twentieth century a very large size was reached, while the plain shoulder-straps were simply de-

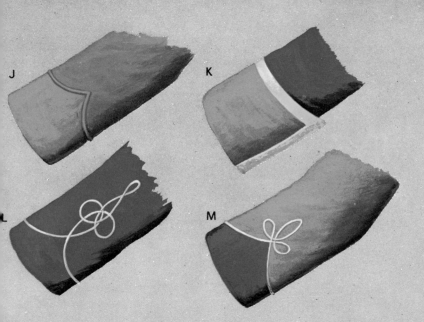

vices to prevent the various belts and slings from slipping off the shoulder.

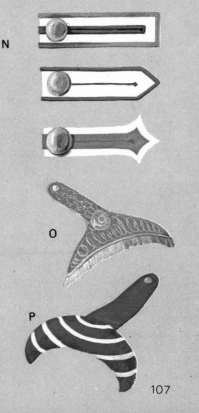

The illustrations on these pages show: (a) French cuff, early eighteenth century; (b) British cuff mid-eighteenth century; (c) British cuff, 1812; (d) French cuff, First Empire; (e) epaulettes (*left to right*): eighteenth century (general pattern), French First Empire and French twentieth century; (f) shoulder-straps, various patterns common to all countries; (g) British cavalry epaulette, mid-nineteenth century; (h) British volunteer's wing, late eighteenth century; (i) German shoulder-strap and drummer's 'swallow's nest', twentieth century; (j) pointed cuff; (k) gaunlet cuff; (l) Austrian knot; (m) crow's-foot cuff, (n) loops (*top to bottom*): square, pointed, bastion; (o) British light infantry officer's wing, early nineteenth century; (p) Dutch-Belgian wing, 1815.

Gunner, Royal Marine Artillery

### The Boxer Rebellion (1900)

The concentrated attacks of Chinese mobs on the European legations in Peking was perhaps one of the earliest opportunities for the forces of different nations to act together against a common enemy, and although there was no supreme command, the ultimate result was successful—the protection of accredited diplomats in a country which could not, or would not, protect them itself.

The 'Boxers' were a Chinese secret society whose ritual is believed to have embraced certain pugilistic attitudes or exercises, and whose doctrine was based upon a hatred of foreign exploiters. In the early summer of 1900 they began their attack on European establishments in Shantung and the neighboring district, killing a number of traders, while

Sepoy, 3rd Sikhs and (*right*) sapper, Bombay Sappers and Miners.

the Manchu court in Peking did nothing to stop the riots. Indeed, even when the German minister-plenipotentiary was murdered, it turned a blind eye. Chinese government troops actually joined with the Boxers in attacking the Peking legations in June.

Shortly German, British and French forces were fighting their way up from the coast. With further molestation threatening the legations, more countries sent contingents to the rescue: Russia, Austria and Italy, to be joined immediately by the Americans and Japanese. The revolt was finally put down in August.

The British contingent included a number of Indian troops sent over from the nearest possible bases. Their uniform, as in the time of the Mutiny, was still largely European in concept, but the headdresses were distinctly native in character; and the Sikhs added a picturesque touch with their impressive beards.

The Sappers and Miners, true to sapper tradition, wore the red tunic of the Royal Engineers, with blue facings — in fact, the Royal Artillery colors in reverse. These colors of red, dark blue and yellow were repeated in the pagri; and the breeches, of dark blue with a scarlet band, were the same as the Gunners'.

The gunner uniform, indeed, was repeated to a great extent in the dress of the Royal Marine Artillery. The Marines, today a single entity, were then divided into Royal Marine Light Infantry in red tunics, and Royal Marine Artillery in blue.

France, also, had a fine body of marine artillery, here dressed very much like their shore brethren. At this period, and until 1914, the characteristic mark of the French gunner was the wide double band of scarlet down the seams of his trousers. The collar and cuffs were red, but in the marine artillery the collar carried an anchor badge. In full dress,

French officers of all arms displayed their rank in an elaborate Austrian knot on both sleeves, carried out in gold or silver thread and reaching well above the elbow.

The Marine Infantry, or Infanterie Coloniale, performed the same duties as the British Marines and, like them, were dressed in the regulation infantry uniform. In this case, however, while the line regiments wore kepis, trousers and epaulettes of red, the Marines' caps were dark blue, their epaulettes yellow and their trousers medium-blue.

The Foreign Legion, too, had been brought up to date, with a uniform identical to that of the infantry of the line, except that the Legion wore a small red grenade on the front of the kepi. Later, the Legion's epaulettes were given a green top as a special distinction.

The longstanding joke about the 'Horse Marines', became a reality in the German contingent of mounted artillerymen

(*Opposite*) private, French marine infantry and officer French marine artillery. (*Right*) non-commissioned officer, German marine artillery.

of precisely that corps. The German Marines wore the black shako of the jägers, and white facings on the tunic.

Colonial troops of the German Empire were clothed in khaki, and wore either the standard pith helmet or a felt hat turned up on the right side.

The German East-Asian Brigade consisted of three infantry regiments, one squadron of light cavalry (Jäger zu Pferd), one field artillery detachment, one company each of pioneers and transport, medical services and three battalions of marines. In the infantry, the regimental number was shown on the shoulder-straps.

The United States Marine Corps at this date wore almost the same uniform as today, allowing for the differences of taste and design. The tunic, in those days, was double-breasted, but the light blue trousers, with their scarlet band, have remained as they were.

On the other hand, the infantry has changed considerably.

Privates of the German East Asia Brigade, 3rd Regiment, and the French Foreign Legion.

Infantry and marine officers of the United States Army.

Here we have the felt hat, almost as that worn in the Cuban War, and a smart khaki outfit much like the British uniform of the same period.

The Italian Army, at the turn of the century, typified the awakening consciousness of a newly united nation barely thirty years old. Italy was taking its place among the important states of Europe, and service in the Army, though compulsory, was considered in the light of a patriotic duty, much as it was in France and Germany.

The infantry of the line, as in most other European armies, was clothed in blue, with a cap of specifically Italian design—neither kepi nor shako. The walking-out dress was smart and sober—and included a pair of white gloves.

On the Japanese side, things had moved rapidly since the country had finally abandoned its policy of hostility to foreigners and foreign influence. Regrettably, in many ways,

Italian infantry private and (*right*) officer, Japanese artillery.

the old traditions were being replaced by Western attitudes. The armed forces were being completely reorganized on the European pattern, with units of the line and an Imperial Guard in the best occidental manner.

As usual, the French Army served as model. The kepi and red trousers had a particular fascination for the Japanese, although for active service they developed a more practical costume of their own.

The infantry consisted of four regiments of the Guard, with two battalions each, and twenty-four line regiments with three battalions each. The uniform here was dark blue throughout, with the facing color (red for the Guard and yellow for the line) displayed on the cap-band and collar.

In the artillery, the establishment consisted of one regiment of artillery of the Guard divided into two batteries each, six regiments of foot artillery, each with three troops of two batteries, and four regiments of coast artillery, of three battalions each. The uniform was the same regulation dark blue, but the facing color was white on the tunics of the Guard, with a red band on their caps. In the line, the white facings were worn on both tunic and cap, and in the coast artillery the same arrangement applied, but in yellow.

The Boxers, of course, wore no recognized uniform, but in the Chinese Army there were signs of Western influence as early as 1897, when some small units appear to have experimented with a uniform of American design: a flat cap with a straight peak and a tunic braided in black.

About 1903, when the Cinese Army took seriously to Western reorganization under European instructors, the uniform assumed a Russian look, with tall leather boots and wide shoulder-straps. The basic color was dark blue, and the headdress vaguely resembled a turban, also in dark blue. The shoulder-straps were in different colors, maybe denoting units, and various Chinese characters appeared on the breast of the tunic. By about 1910, the turban-type head-dress had been abandoned in favor of a peaked cap.

Chinese 'Boxer'

Russian gunner, horse artillery.

### The Russo-Japanese War (1904–05)

Russia and Japan were both trying to extend their sphere of influence: Russia to the east, Japan to the west. A clash was inevitable.

Japan resented the fact that half the island of Saghalien had been ceded to Russia, and Russia needed Port Arthur, on the Chinese mainland, as an ice-free harbor for the extension of the Trans-Siberian Railway. Negotiation proved fruitless, and diplomatic relations were severed on February 6, 1904.

Russia was unprepared and apathetic—almost indifferent to the cause and object of the war. In the East she had 80,000 guards and patrols along the railroad, and the garrisons of Port Arthur and Vladivostok. Japan had a first-line army of 270,000 men; but Russia, on the other hand, with her enormous population, could draw on almost unlimited reserves.

Naval operations, as may be expected, initiated the fighting. Japanese torpedo-boats from Admiral Togo's battle fleet made

Russian troops. (*Above*) private, 1st Regiment Lithuania, and officer, 12th Dragoons (undress).

a daring raid on the Russian Squadron in Port Arthur harbor; later the Russian admiral Makarov went out to pursue the Japanese ships. This was perhaps the earliest occasion on which explosive mines were laid in enemy waters; it was certainly the first instance of naval warfare in the modern sense. The Russians, perhaps more by good luck than good navigation, managed to avoid the danger, but on the way back, one of their best ships, the *Petropavlovsk,* struck a mine and sank with the admiral and 200 men on board.

The Russian Army had undergone a measure of reorganization in 1882, when all the cavalry except the Guard was converted to dragoons. Thus, the colorful hussars and lancers ceased to exist until 1910, when they emerged again in their full splendor. The Cossacks, of course, were unaffected.

The artillery was still wearing the dark green uniform

with red piping and shoulder-straps, and black collars and cuffs for the officers. In the horse artillery, the dress was the same except that the breeches were blue, while in the field artillery they were dark green, like the tunic.

In the infantry the standard dark green was in wear: tunic, tall boots and small fur caps for dress occasions. For undress, a flat round cap, without a peak, was worn.

The Japanese love of color was reflected in the dress of the cavalry and the military bands. The cavalry of the Guard wore a very dark blue jacket, laced hussar-fashion in scarlet, with brass buttons and scarlet piping. The full-dress shako was scarlet, with a short red-over-white plume, and the scarlet breeches had a light green band stitched down the sides.

In the line, the dress was similar, except that the scarlet was replaced by white (in the jacket and cap) and on the breeches a white piping replaced the green stripes. The shako was black throughout, with a white-over-red plume.

The military bands were particularly resplendent. There were two companies of these, one for the

Officer, Japanese cavalry of the Guard.

Japanese troops. Gunner, Coast artillery and (*right*) private, infantry of the Guard.

Guard and the other for the line. Both companies were dressed in the regulation dark blue tunic, but their shakos and trousers were scarlet colored.

Rank badges for officers were akin to the French system of large Austrian knots of gold or silver thread on the sleeves, but in a somewhat simplified version. For the non-commissioned officers, a system of straight bars of lace was in force, worn at right angles to the edge of the sleeve. These bands were in arm-of-service color, and set just above the cuff.

The war dragged on, with varying successes on either side. Peace was eventually signed on September 5, 1905, through the mediation of the President of the United States and the influence of the United States, Britain and Germany. By this war, Japan gained a position as a world power.

## The Italo-Turkish War (1911–12)

With Italian influence gradually expanding as a result of the colonization of Eritrea and the founding of various commercial ventures in the Turkish possession of Tripolitania, sooner or later the newcomers were bound to come into conflict with the Porte. When the Young Turks assumed power in Constantinople, the situation worsened: Italian enterprise was hampered, especially in Tripolitania, until by December 1910, it was clear that some kind of assurances were needed.

In July 1911 Rome informed Constantinople that if matters did not improve, military preparations would begin on September 20. In reply, the Turks sent arms to Tripoli. Italy declared war on September 29.

The Italian Bersaglieri were soon involved. On October 23, two companies were attacked in an oasis near Tripoli when Turks and Arabs advanced in force. They were beaten off,

Italian troops. Trooper, Libyan cavalry, ánd a bersagliere.

Trooper, Turkish lancers of the Guard.

but the Bersaglieri were cut to pieces by natives who had inflitrated their lines. These troops were the light infantry of the Italian Army, and in full dress wore a very picturesque hat, well tilted to the right and decorated with an impressive plume of falling cock-tail feathers.

Native units of colonial troops were also beginning to appear, clothed in uniforms based upon a keen regard for Oriental dress.

On the Turkish side, an astrakhan fez was the distinctive headdress for the cavalry and artillery. It was worn with a dark blue tunic and gray breeches with a scarlet band, while the facing color appeared in the pointed cuffs and the collar-patch. The Ertogrul Leib-Regiment wore the same, except that the collar was uniformly red, the cuffs were straight with a red cuff-slash and the breeches were dark blue. In addition, there was a red plastron buttoned over the front of the tunic.

Peace was finally signed between the two countries at Ouchy, near Lausanne, on October 14, 1912, Turkey recognizing the Italian annexations in Africa, and Italy restoring the Aegean Islands to Turkey.

121

## The Balkan Wars (1912–13)

In 1912, the Ottoman Empire extended as far west as the Adriatic and included many territories which were ethnologically foreign to their Turkish rulers. Turkey, weakened by her recent war with Italy, was therefore ripe for attack by sundry Balkan nations anxious to regain their lost provinces. In the autumn of that year, a state of tension gradually built up, until on October 17, the kingdoms of Bulgaria, Serbia and Greece declared war on Turkey. Montenegro joined them shortly afterward, actually starting the fighting.

At the turn of the century, the Greek artillery was equipped with 12-pounder and 9-pounder Krupp guns, which were presumably still in use in 1912. The uniform of this arm included the French type of overalls, with false boots of leather, and a red plume for full dress, also copied from the French artillery.

Greek Army uniforms: Evzone and private, infantry of the line.

122

A gunner of the Greek Army.

The most picturesque of the Greek troops were the Evzones, or light infantry, who have survived in their traditional costume to the present day as the Royal Guard in Athens. Sources disagree as to their exact uniform, and even contemporary photographs seldom show two figures dressed alike. There were eight battalions, and the explanation may be that every battalion had its own version of the dress.

The infantry of the line consisted of ten regiments in the early years of the century. They were dressed in a sober dark blue tunic, with red facings, and light gray trousers. At this period they carried the Gras rifle, with thirty-eight rounds in the pouches and forty-eight in the haversack. The cavalry was small in numbers, namely eight regiments only, dressed in olive green with crimson facings.

The Turks were in an unenviable position, having to fight on three fronts simultaneously: on the Bulgarian frontier in Thrace, on the Greek frontier in Macedonia and on the Serbo-Bulgarian border.

The Serbs, reinforced by one Bulgarian division, attacked

Serbian cavalry trooper.

the lines of the River Vardar and enveloped Scutari and Monastir, while the Greeks concentrated on Salonika, against which a Bulgarian divison was also advancing.

The Serbian uniform was more 'national' in character than the Greeks' (apart from the Evzones), for although the tunic was of the plain universal pattern, the cap and footwear were distinctly indigenous. This, of course, applied chiefly to the service dress of 1912, for in the years immediately preceding the war, we find that full dress, here too, succumbed to the French influence—or maybe was even imitated at third hand from the Russians of the 1890's, who had adopted the kepi for many of their units.

In 1901, however, this was exchanged for a fur cap of Russian appearance, and the dark blue tunic was decorated with red facings. Trousers were black for full dress, but blue-gray for field service wear.

Serbian artillery gunner and infantry private.

The Serbian cavalry was probably dressed in khaki for active service, but devoid of the dark blue collars and shoulder-straps (the latter bearing the regimental number) which characterized the former light blue tunics.

The Bulgarian divisions were well up to strength: they were, in fact, large formations of some 20,000 men each, which meant that the Bulgarian Army could put about 180,000 men in the field. In addition, there were two divisions of similar strength in reserve.

In the original plan, six of the active divisions were to be allocated to the Eastern front, with their objectives as Lule Burgas and ultimately Constantinople. The remaining three were to cooperate with the Serbs against Macedonia; but at the last minute the Bulgarian High Command decided to alter this arrangement by keeping eight divisions for the Eastern front and employing no more than one on the Western.

This may have been a sound decision strategically, because while the Turks could be reinforced in Macedonia, to do so in Thrace was quite a different proposition. However, the Serbs took a different view. They felt themselves to some extent abandoned by their ally and began to harbor a measure of resentment which was to break out, in the following year, into open conflict.

The Bulgarian Army was dressed in a distinctly Russian style as a result, no doubt, of the influence exercised by the Russian instructors who officered the Bulgarian legion of volunteers formed in 1877 at Bucharest and Ploesti. The small fur cap and tall boots, in particular, were a close copy, but in this case the cap badge was a brass Bulgarian Cross.

At the turn of the century, there were four cavalry regiments in Bulgaria, in dark blue uniforms with scarlet collars, cuffs and shoulder-straps. The regiments were distinguished by the color of the piping on the tunic and breeches: thus the

Trooper, Bulgarian 3rd Cavalry Regiment.

1st regiment wore white; the 2nd, red; the 3rd, yellow; and the 4th, light blue.

The infantry uniform was dark green, with the regimental facing color shown on shoulder-straps, cuff-slashes and piping (e.g. white for 'Ferdinand' Regiment, light blue for 'Clementine', red for 'Alexander').

In the artillery, the dark green tunic was worn, but with a black collar and pointed cuffs in the same color. The breeches were dark blue and the piping was red.

For summer wear in the field an entirely white uniform was designed, again unquestionably based on the Russian model, but now worn with a white peaked cap.

Officers' ranks were denoted by the number of stars on the epaulettes or shoulder-straps; and in full dress a silver sash with green and red strands was worn. Commanding officers of regiments and those of higher rank wore the same sash with the addition of large tassels hanging on the side.

Bulgarian artillery officer; private, Bulgarian Clementine Infantry Regiment.

127

Turkish light infantry sergeant.

Montenegro was one of Europe's smallest states, originally a principality in its own right with a small army of militiamen. When it became a kingdom in 1910, however, a more modern army was organized and clothed in gray, except for the Royal Escort which wore a picturesque uniform based on the national dress of the country.

The arms of service were denoted by the color of the piping on the shoulder-straps as follows: infantry, scarlet; machine-gun corps, light blue; artillery, yellow; engineers, red. General officers were distinguished by dark red facings, and if surprise may be felt that such ranks existed in so small an army, it must be remembered that all Montenegrins from the age of fourteen were liable for military service for the remainder of their lives. It is recorded, therefore, that in 1910, the country could have as many as 38,000 men under arms, out of a population of no more than 300,000.

The Turkish Army was still clothed in the uniform that was in wear during the Italian conflict, at all events as far as full dress was concerned.

In the infantry, this consisted of a dark blue tunic and

trousers, with a scarlet fez for headdress. The line regiments wore scarlet collar-patches, shoulder-straps, cuff-slashes and piping, but in the light infantry the facing color for the tunic was dark green.

Badges of rank for non-commissioned officers took the form of large chevrons in the facing color, worn on the left sleeve, and based approximately on the same pattern as the British.

After the peace was signed in London on May 30, 1913, most of Turkey in Europe was partitioned among Bulgaria, Serbia and Greece, the larger portion going to Bulgaria. But some parts remained in dispute, resulting in a new outbreak between the former allies, Bulgaria striking first without warning. Peace was signed this time in Bucharest on August 10, 1913, Bulgaria losing most of her earlier gains.

Montenegrin troops. Royal Escort and infantry of the line privates.

## World War I (1914–18)

Less than a year after the Balkan Wars came to an end further trouble in that disturbed peninsula resulted in the most all-embracing and far-reaching conflict so far experienced.

Several provinces of the Austro-Hungarian Empire were inhabited by a Serbian-speaking population harboring a small number of malcontents, some of whom were organized in secret societies. On June 28, 1914, the Archduke Franz-Ferdinand, heir to the Imperial Throne, on a State visit to Sarajevo in Bosnia, was assassinated by members of one of these societies.

Austria reacted quickly, demanding satisfaction from Serbia, who promptly sought the aid of Russia. This was the opportunity that Germany had been waiting for. As Austria's ally she was bound to oppose any move by Russia, who in turn was allied to France.

Diplomatic breakdowns, threats and counter-threats crisscrossed over Europe in quick succession until at last the whole situation exploded on August 3, 1914. France and Germany had declared war, and Germany, in order to outflank her age-old enemy, thought nothing of attacking a

British Army uniforms of the World War I period. The staff sergeant (*left*) is of the Royal Scots Greys, the only mounted regiment in the British Army to wear the bearskin cap.

neutral and almost defenseless Belgium. Great Britain, as a guarantor of Belgian neutrality, immediately sent an ultimatum to Germany—which, of course, was rejected; on August 4, Britain found herself at war with the German Empire.

The German Government had gambled on British neutrality; but the shock was not severe, since the 'contemptible little army' could be destroyed with ease. It was even crossing the Channel openly to invite such destruction at little cost to the Germans.

The British Army went out in the now familiar khaki field service dress, wearing the 1908 web equipment and armed with the short magazine Lee-Enfield rifle which proved so deadly to the Germans.

The regular army was supplemented by a large number of

Trooper, the Australian Light Horse, 1914.

volunteer units organized as infantry battalions of the Territorial Force and Yeomanry regiments of cavalry. Most Territorial units were attached to county regiments as additional battalions, but in London they were either line or rifle regiments in their own right. Many of these, such as the Honourable Artillery Company were of ancient lineage, and the 11th London (The Finsbury Rifles) even claimed descent from the Finsbury Archers of the Middle Ages, although a direct line has never been fully established.

The Royal Scots Greys (2nd Dragoons) is the only mounted regiment in the British Army to wear the bearskin cap, and the only Scottish regiment of regular cavalry. Their badge of the Napoleonic Eagle commemorates the remarkable feat of Sergeant Ewart at Waterloo when he captured the Eagle of the French 45th Regiment of the line.

It was not long before all the overseas countries of the Empire were sending men and equipment in loyal support of the Mother Country: the Australians and New Zealanders who made history at Gallipoli; the Canadians of Vimy Ridge; the South Africans in their own country, under General Smuts, a former enemy; the magnificent Indian Army in several theaters of war—all came unhesitatingly to swell the ranks of Britain and her allies. Apart from its own regular troops, almost every Dominion had a number of Scottish units, most of them allied to a parent regiment in Scotland.

Some of the finest fighting men came from the native regiments: the Nigeria Regiment and the King's African Rifles; the Sikhs and Punjabis of the Indian Army; the wiry little Gurkhas of Nepal, to name but a few.

The Australian Light Horse were volunteers who provided their own mounts. There were twenty-three regiments of this branch, all dressed in the same uniform, without any apparent regimental distinctions.

When the French Army mobilized for war, it went out in

Officer, the New Brunswick Scottish, 1914, and (*right*) the King's African Rifles, 1918.

the campaign dress then in wear: the blue greatcoat in the infantry and the blue tunic in the cavalry and artillery. It was the only army to retain bright colors in the field, and the red trousers of the French contrasted oddly with the drab khaki of the 'Tommies'. The red kepi, however, was now covered with a blue cap-cover for war.

The chasseurs, on the other hand, were not concerned with vivid colors. Their uniform was dark blue and their trousers gray, which they wore with the regulation kepi for the *bataillons de plaine* and a dark blue beret for the mountain battalions. These were the famous Chasseurs Alpins who fought in the Vosges and earned for themselves the nickname of the 'Blue Devils'. The beret, today worn with the bugle-horn to the right, was then worn with the badge on the left, as in the present-day British army. By tradition, the chasseur was tough: he could outmarch any mere infantryman of the line, and the monumental pack which he carried was rivalled only by the Zóuaves.

French troops, 1914. Alpine chasseur and a private, infantry of the line

134

Trooper, French dragoons, 1914

The French infantry was armed with the Lebel rifle, which carried a built-in magazine in front of the trigger-guard, thus imparting an unusually bulky appearance to that part of the weapon. When marching at the 'slope', it was carried high on the right shoulder, trigger to the front. The bayonet was long and narrow, triangular in cross-section and fitted with a hooked crossbar.

The cavalry consisted mainly of cuirassiers, dragoons, hussars and chasseurs. At the outset, all arms wore the modified full dress that served as service dress, with the cuirasses and helmets covered in khaki cloth to avoid reflections; but here too the regulation red breeches were retained.

In full dress the dragoon helmet differed from that of the cuirassiers in that it did not carry the small black tuft at the tip of the comb. The large trefoils worn in lieu of epaulettes were common to all cavalry branches except the cuirassiers, who had red epaulettes. The collar, in the dragoons, was white for all regiments, who were distinguished solely by the white numeral on a dark blue collar-patch.

In some units of light cavalry a new helmet had been authorized, similar in design to the dragoons', to replace the shako; but few issues had been made by the time the war broke out. The hussars' shako was sky-blue, with a white Austrian knot in front and a plume of cock-tail feathers, while the chasseurs' version was the same, but with a brass bugle-horn badge and a spherical ball-tuft. The tunic was sky-blue in both branches, with white metal buttons and hussar-type lacing (white for the hussars and black for the chasseurs). The regimental number was shown on the collar, which in the hussars was of the same color as the tunic.

(*Below*) French troops, 1914: officer, 19th Chasseurs a Cheval, and artillery gunner.

The chasseurs' collar and cuff-slashes were red.

The French artillery had kept its dark blue uniform with the characteristic double band of scarlet down the seams of the trousers: a distinction it had enjoyed since the late 1820's. The field branch was equipped with that splendid weapon, the 75mm. quick-firing gun, whose breech-mechanism was a masterpiece of mechanical design.

Service dress in the French army had altered little since 1870, but as the war progressed and replacements became necessary, the old uniform was scrapped and an entirely new design evolved. The general cut remained the same, but the color was changed to 'horizon-blue' for all arms—a color which was supposed to merge into the landscape. Puttees, on the British model, were issued, and about 1916 a steel helmet appeared, painted blue-gray, and easily the most handsome of the necessary but unattractive headdresses produced by the various belligerent countries. It carried a small comb on the top and was secured by a brown leather chinstrap

Private, French infantry of the line, 1917.

which fastened over the front peak of the helmet when not in use. The badge on the front took the form of a grenade in the artillery and infantry of the line, and a bugle-horn in all branches of chasseurs.

The potential strength of the Russian army was enormous. It was confidently expected to 'steam-roller' the Germans on the Eastern Front by sheer weight of numbers, and indeed when it gained several initial successes in East Prussia everybody thought that Berlin lay within easy reach. But the Germans had planned their retreat well: the Russians were pushed back on the rebound, and with the Austrians helping in Galicia, the whole front settled down to the same static warfare as in the West.

A new uniform had been designed for the Russian Army in 1913: a brilliant conception which could enable plain service dress to be transformed to full dress by the simple process of buttoning on a colored plastron and attaching the appropriate collar and cuffs. These articles were yellow for

Privates, Russian infantry of the line, 1914.

grenadier units and crimson for the jägers or light infantry. In the infantry of the line, various colorings appeared, such as red, blue, white and green-black, the last three being piped in red.

The cap was made of gray lambskin, with a khaki top, and some regiments bore the small brass scroll which was worn as a battle-honor. Officers' breeches had red piping stitched down the seams. Most of the troops were dressed in the light khaki shirt-tunic, with its high collar, which was typical of the Russian Army at this period. It was worn with a peaked cap of the same color, usually well tilted to the right.

The greatcoat was carried bandolier-fashion on the left shoulder, with the ends tucked into a brass mess-tin. There was no pack, but instead a large leather-bound haversack was worn on the left hip, balanced by a smaller variety worn on the right hip.

Full dress uniforms were particularly resplendent, especially in the Guard, which comprised the Emperor's bodyguards

Russian troops, 1914. Sergeant, 1st Siberian Jägers, and officer, horse artillery of the Garde du Corps.

139

and escorts, regiments of cuirassiers, dragoons, lancers, hussars and cossacks, as well as infantry, artillery and the ancillary services. The distinctive shako, peculiar to the Russian Army, appears to be an interesting modification of the bell-topped model of the early nineteenth century. It was worn in the infantry of the Guard as well as in the artillery.

The Belgian Army, led by that resolute young monarch King Albert I, put up stout resistance against the German onslaught. However, the Belgians were heavily outnumbered and in spite of British support had to fall back to the Yser.

In general, the Belgian uniforms resembled the French, except for the red trousers. The cavalry branch included two regiments of guides, four of lancers, and two of mounted chasseurs, all in hussar-type tunics with different colored lacing according to the regiments. Thus, the guides had a green tunic

Belgian Army uniforms of 1914. Trooper, 4th Lancers.

light
infantry

artillery
officer

with a crimson collar and pointed cuffs, and bright yellow lacing, while the breeches were crimson with two yellow stripes. The lancers were in blue, with blue-gray breeches. Regimental distinctions were shown by the color of the collar, cuffs and lance-cap top: 1st, crimson; 2nd, yellow; 3rd, white; 4th, ultramarine. Further, the lacing on the tunic was white for Regiments 1 and 2 and yellow for 3 and 4.

In the chasseurs, the colorings were a yellow shako, collar and cuffs for the 1st Regiment, and the same in scarlet for the 2nd.

The artillery was much like the French in appearance, but instead of a kepi wore a small black busby with a scarlet bag. The epaulettes were red for non-commissioned officers and other ranks, gold or gold-and-silver (according to rank) for officers, and yellow for trumpeters.

The infantry was divided into line regiments, grenadiers, chasseurs and carabiniers. The line regiments wore a double-breasted tunic with brass buttons and pointed cuffs outlined with red piping. The collar was red and the trousers gray with red piping. The headdress

141

was a black shako with yellow fittings and a red ball-tuft and plume. Later in the war a French-type uniform was adopted for the whole Belgian army, but in khaki.

The United States did not enter the war until April 2, 1917, when indiscriminate sinkings of American shipping by German U-boats prompted Congress to declare war on the Central Powers. This was much in the Allies' favor, because the Americans would now reinforce the Western Front to counter the vast influx of man-power released from the Eastern Front following the collapse of Russia a few months earlier.

For service in France, the United States Army wore the khaki service dress of the period, but full dress was still in wear at home. The khaki uniform resembled the British in some respects, such as the identical steel helmet. For ordinary wear, however, the felt hat served for all ranks, no longer dented lengthwise in the manner of a civilian 'trilby' but with four dents on the model of the Royal Canadian Mounted Police, and fitted with a light blue cord in the infantry.

Arm-of-service badges

Artillery trumpeter, 1914.

United States troops. Machine-gun sergeant and private, 1917.

were worn in the shape of a bronze button on the left collar-end (i.e. swords in the cavalry, guns in the artillery and rifles in the infantry). The button on the other side was stamped with the initials US and the regimental number.

Since 1912, the Serbian Army had enjoyed little respite. Conversely, the experience gained in the Balkan wars had turned it into a seasoned and well-organized force. The initial Austrian attack was met with resilience and although the primary retreat was arduous, the counter-offensive and re-capture of Belgrade in December 1914 did much to restore morale. At the start of the war Serbian uniforms had not changed much since 1912.

Italy, too, had recent campaign experience when she declared war on Austria-Hungary (but not Germany) on May 20, 1915. The theater of operations was in Northern Italy, mostly in the Trentino. An Austrian offensive on the Isonzo was repulsed in 1916, but on October 24, 1917 the disaster of Caporetto nearly proved fatal. However, exactly one year later to the day, the Italian Army gained the final and decisive victory of Vittorio Veneto.

The Italian field uniform was gray-green in color, and the steel helmet was of the French pattern, painted gray-green. The Bersaglieri wore this dress, with the cock-tail feathers on the helmet for special occasions; of course, full dress was still in force in peace time. Another characteristic Italian body was the Alpini—a counterpart of the French chasseurs alpins—mountain troops wearing a felt hat with a single feather on the left.

Serbian cavalry officer, 1914 and Portuguese infantry private, 1917.

The Japanese Army had been further modernized since the Russo-Japanese war. However, its contribution to the Allied war effort was limited, resolving itself principally in the siege of Ts'ing-tao and the despatch of a brigade to Singapore at the British request in 1916. It also furnished an effective guard for the Trans-Siberian Railway between Vladivostok and Lake Baikal in 1917.

Portugal came into the war in March 1916 as a result of a declaration of war by Germany, who had already made some desultory attacks on Portuguese territory in Africa. Indeed, the main war effort of Portugal was concentrated in that continent, although she did send a token force to the Western Front. These troops were clothed in horizon-blue and wore a

Italian bersagliere, 1916; Japanese infantry private, 1914.

helmet resembling the British, except for the corrugated appearance of the pressed steel in the Portuguese version. In effect, the Portuguese looked like a British soldier dyed blue, much as the Belgian looked like a Frenchman dyed khaki.

The peace-time German uniforms were varied and colorful, especially in the cavalry, and the existence of a number of states in the Empire, each with its own military organization, makes the study of German uniforms an extremely interesting subject.

The German troops set out in the brand new field-gray service dress. Colored piping and similar ornaments had not yet been considered unsuitable, and every effort was made to retain some measure of traditional appearance.

In full dress, however, the matter was easily resolved. Generally speaking, every regiment, of whatever country, proclaimed its identity in the facing color. Thus, the 35th Brandenburg Infantry Regiment was dressed in the regulation

German troops, 1914. Officer, 35th Brandenburg Infantry Regiment in service dress, and drummer, Bavarian Leib Regiment.

Trooper, Prussian 9th Uhlans, 1914

dark blue tunic and black trousers with a red collar, shoulder straps and cuff-slashes, and the regimental number in yellow on the shoulder-straps, while a white piping surrounded the cuff-slashes.

The cavalry consisted of cuirassiers, dragoons, hussars, uhlans and *Jäger zu Pferde* (mounted rifles). In addition, there were chevauleger regiments in Bavaria (in place of uhlans) and regiments of heavy cavalry in Saxony and Bavaria (in place of cuirassiers). The cuirassiers were in white as before, and the dragoons in light blue. The hussars wore red, black, brown, green or light blue according to the regiment, and the uhlans were distinguished mainly by the color of the plastron. They wore the conventional lance-cap, but in Bavaria, as chevaulegers, the pickelhaube was their headdress, and their uniforms were dark green.

The infantry side-drums were of a very shallow pattern

introduced in 1854 and carried from a fastening on the waist-belt. The stretchers consisted of five screws, distributed around the circumference, and the hoops were decorated with twenty-five triangles. There was no Royal Guard in Bavaria, but the Leib-Infanterie Regiment served that purpose. The Bavarian uniform was basically light blue throughout, for the infantry regiments at any rate, of which there were twenty-three, apart from the Life Regiment.

The jäger were the light infantry of the German Army, dressed in the dark green tunics traditional to that corps. The 10th Battalion was apparently descended from a unit which had seen service at Gibraltar and wore that battle-honor on the cuff, an honor shared by Hanoverian Infantry Regiments Nos. 73 and 79. The light infantry branch was represented in the Prussian Guard by two battalions: the Garde-Jäger Bataillon and the Garde-Schützen Bataillon, the latter being originally the rifle battalion raised at Neuchâtel, in Switzerland, after the Napoleonic wars, mostly from survivors of Berthier's yellow-coated Bataillon de Neuchâtel.

Most of the German artillery wore the regulation dark blue tunic with black collar and cuffs. The shoulder-straps were in different colors, usually scarlet, white or light blue, while the helmet aways carried the ball ornament. In the two Bavarian foot artillery regiments, however, the helmet was fitted with a spike as in the infantry. The Saxon artillery was dressed in green, with scarlet collar and cuffs, but otherwise the general pattern conformed to the Prussian model.

With the war dragging on year after year, and with the British blockade proving increasingly effective, the German need for metal resulted first in the removal of the spikes and other ornaments from the helmets. Next, the helmets were discarded altogether and replaced by the ugliest, although doubtlessly the most efficient trench helmet ever devised: the 'coal scuttle' which survived until 1945.

The service dress of the Austro-Hungarian Army was of a light gray-green color officially described as *hechtgrau* (pike-gray), but full dress, especially in the cavalry was colorful

German Army uniforms, 1914. Private, Prussian 10th Jäger Battalion, and (*right*) gunner, 32nd Saxon Field Artillery Regiment.

as well as picturesque, by reason of the slung coat which was worn pelisse-fashion over the left shoulder by all mounted units, even the transport corps.

The chevaulegers had been disbanded in 1852, and the cuirassiers in 1868, thus leaving the dragoons, hussars and uhlans to represent the Austrian cavalry. An interesting feature was that by now the uhlans no longer carried lances.

Hungary is the home of the hussar; therefore it is not surprising that this arm, with its sixteen regiments, formed the bulk of the Imperial and Royal cavalry in 1914. There were also several Hungarian second-line (*honvéd*) hussar regiments dressed in blue tunics and pelisses with red lacing and white fur, with the regimental identity, in this case, shown by the color of the shako.

Austro-Hungarian troops, 1914. Artillery gunner and infantry officer.

The dragoons continued to wear the handsome black helmet with its large comb curving over the top, and in this branch the regiments were denoted by the color of the collar, cuffs and piping on the light blue tunic. The same color was used for the uhlans' tunic, but here the regimental facing color appeared in the lance-cap only. In all three arms the breeches were red. The traditional brown coat of the Austrian gunners remained in wear, with red facings as before, worn with blue trousers.

In the infantry, the characteristic white coat was exchanged for a more serviceable blue tunic in 1868. This garment showed the regimental facing color on the collar, shoulder-straps, cuffs and small pads, or rolls, set at the base of the shoulderstraps.

The Bosnian infantry, as Mohammedans, wore a scarlet fez of Turkish pattern, and knee-breeches, while the light infantry—the Kaiserjäger—were dressed in pike-gray with a black felt hat decorated with a large plume of cocktail feathers. These were mountain troops operating in the same manner as the Italian Alpini and the French

Austro-Hungarian cavalry: trooper, 11th Hussars, 1914.

chasseurs alpins.

It was not only Austria-Hungary whose friendship Germany had actively cultivated, but for years the Ottoman Empire had been openly courted as well. A senior German officer had been lent to the Porte to reorganize the Turkish Army; German arms and equipment were being supplied, and it is therefore not surprising that the Turkish Army assisted the German ships *Breslau* and *Goeben* to bombard Odessa in the autumn of 1914. This, naturally enough, resulted in a declaration of war by the allies in November.

The Turks operated first in the Caucasus against the Russians, and later were successful in forcing Allenby to surrender at Kut-el-Amara, while also repelling the Allied landings at Gallipoli. In Palestine, however, they were not so fortunate, for on December 9, 1917, the keys of Jerusalem were handed over without struggle to a rather surprised sergeant of the St. Pancras Rifles, and on October 30, 1918, with her allies crumbling on all sides, Turkey asked for an Armistice.

The Turkish Army was clothed in khaki service dress with a curious type of helmet

Private, Bulgarian infantry of the line, 1917.

Turkish engineer officer, 1914, and private, Turkish infantry
of the line, 1916.

devoid of a front peak—a concession to the religious belief of
the Muslims who must not shade their eyes from the sun.

The remaining ally of the Central Powers was Bulgaria,
who was really in no shape to undertake another war after
being so soundly beaten a few years earlier. However, pressure
was brought to bear on her and she declared war on Serbia
in October 1915. Whether this intervention was effective or
not is problematical; but in any case it served to swell the
numbers on the side of the Germans and Austrians, besides
tying down important Allied forces in the Balkans. In Bulgaria
herself, opposition to the war was widespread.

The Bulgarian troops, still wearing a uniform predom-
inantly Russian in design, were now dressed in khaki. Some
units were also supplied with German field-gray clothing,
worn with Bulgarian badges and shoulder-straps; and the
equipment was entirely German. It is interesting to note, however, that in many cases the national footwear was in use,
although probably unofficially.

153

# GLOSSARY

**Aiguillettes:** Ornamental cords, usually gold, terminating in small metal tags, worn mostly at the right shoulder.

**Arm of service:** A somewhat loose term denoting the various branches of an army.

**Austrian Knot:** Sometimes called 'Hungarian knot'. An ornamental pattern of cording, usually worn on the cuff, arranged in two large rings flanking a taller pointed shape in the center.

**Bearskin Cap:** The large bearskin headdress worn by grenadiers.

**Bell-topped Shako:** A shako (q.v.) broader at the top than at the bottom.

**Busby:** A fur headdress, smaller than a bearskin, worn by hussars and sometimes horse artillery. It nearly always carried a colored cloth top which fell to the side (busby-bag) and was often decorated with an upright plume, either in front or at the side.

**Cantinière:** In the French army, the woman who attended to the regimental canteen. Originally little more than a camp-follower, dressed in cast-off items of uniform, she gradually acquired status and eventually achieved official recognition on the ration-strength of her unit.

**Cap-Lines:** The more or less ornamental cords which connected a headdress with the body. Sometimes called 'body-lines'.

**Chasseurs:** French light infantry. (Ger. *Jäger*).

**Chechia:** A Zouave's headdress. A red cap with a black tassel, somewhat resembling a fez, but cylindrical in shape and not rigid.

**Cockade:** A rosette worn on the headdress. From the eighteenth century onward it denoted the country (e.g., black for Great Britain, white for France) and later displayed the national colors.

**Comb:** The curved plate of upright metal surmounting a helmet. (Germ.: *Bügel*).

**Crest:** A fur ornament, usually surmounting the comb. (Fr.: *chenille*. Ger.: *Raupe*).

**Crow's Foot:** An ornamental pattern of cording, usually worn on the cuff, forming a trefoil of three rings.

**Cuff-Slash:** The upright strip of cloth, usually bearing three buttons, worn over a straight cuff.

**Czapka:** A Polish lance-cap.

**Dolman:** A hussar jacket or tunic, ornamented on the front with a varying number of loops or lacing.

**Epaulette:** A detachable shoulder-piece formed by a strap widening out as a crescent over the top of the shoulder and decorated with a fringe. Where the fringe is absent it is sometimes termed a counter-epaulette.

**Facings:** The parts of a uniform, such as collar, cuffs and lapels which are different in color from the main garment.

**Flank Companies:** The grenadier and light companies of an infantry battalion. (Fr.: *compagnies d'elite*).

**Field Officer:** A major, lieutenant-colonel or colonel.

**Gorget:** The last relic of armor. A metal crescent-shaped plate worn at the throat by officers.

**Hackle:** A short upright plume.

**Kepi:** A French soldier's peaked cap, normally smaller at the top than at the base.

**Kurtka:** A Polish lancer's tunic, fitted with a plastron (q.v.). (Germ.: *Ulanka*).

**Lace, Regimental:** In the British army, the white strips with colored lines (different from regiment to regiment) which decorated the jackets of corporals and other ranks. Sergeants wore white lace and officers either gold or silver.

**Loop:** The lace surrounding a button-hole.

**Matross:** In the early days of artillery, a common gunner.

**Mirliton:** A tall conical headdress, without a peak, and wound around with a spiral of colored cloth.

**Overalls:** Long trousers with an under-boot strap or chain, worn by mounted men. Originally designed for service dress but nowadays worn in a very tight-fitting version on dress occasions.

**Pagri:** An Indian's turban.

**Pelisse:** The fur-trimmed coat carried by hussars, slung over the left shoulder when not in wear.

**Pickelhaube:** Literally, 'spike-bonnet'. The Germans' slang term for their helmet.

**Plastron:** The cloth front buttoned over a lancer's kurtka to act as a wind-cheater.

**Poshteen:** A sneepskin jerkin worn by Indian troops.

**Rifle:** A firearm with a grooved, or rifled barrel, imparting a spin to the bullet.

**Shoulder-Straps:** Cloth shoulder-pieces, buttoning near the collar, originally intended to keep the shoulder-belts in position.

**Sepoy:** An Indian infantryman.

**Shako:** A rigid peaked headdress, which may be cylindrical, conical or bell-topped (q.v.) in shape.

**Swallows'-Nests:** Cloth shoulder-ornaments, usually laced, denoting bandsmen. Worn mostly in Germany.

**Sword-Knot:** The strap attached to a sword-hilt, serving to secure the weapon to the soldier's wrist. (Fr.: *dragonne*. Germ.: *Faustriemen*).

**Turban:** The cloth or skin surrounding the base of a helmet.

**Turnbacks:** The turned-over part of the coat-tails.

**Wings:** Shoulder-ornaments in the form of a large crescent usually denoting bandsmen and (in the British army) flank companies (q.v.).

## PLACES TO VISIT

United States Military Academy
  Museum, West Point, New York
Fort Ticonderoga Museum, Ticonderoga, New York
Gettysburg National Military Park, Gettysburg, Pennsylvania
Newport Artillery Company Museum, Newport, Rhode Island
Castle Museum, York, England
Imperial War Museum, London, England
Royal United Services Museum, Edinburgh, Scotland
Regimental Museums in Great Britain
Heeresgeschichtliches Museum, Vienna, Austria
Musée Royal de l'Armée, Brussels, Belgium
Historisches Museum, Rastatt, Germany
Leger-en Wapenmuseum, Leyden, Germany
Musée de l'Armée, Paris, France
Musée Historique, Strasbourg, France
Schweizerisches Nazionalmuseum, Zurich, Switzerland
Musée du Chateau, Colombier, Switzerland
The Army Museum, Halifax, Nova Scotia
South African National War Museum, Johannesburg, South Africa

# BOOKS TO READ

*A Pageant of America.* R. H. Gabriel, (ed). Yale University Press, 1937.
*Military Uniforms in Color.* Preben Kannik. Macmillan, 1968.
*Encyclopaedia Britannica,* 11th edition, London, 1910.
*European Military Uniforms.* Paul Martin. Spring Books, London, 1967.
*History of the British Army.* Sir John Fortescue. Macmillan, 1910.
*British Military Uniforms.* W. Y. Carman. Spring Books, London, 1968.
*A History of the Uniforms of the British Army.* C. C. P. Lawson. (4 Vols.) Norman Publications, London, 1961–1966.
*Indian Army Uniforms.* W. Y. Carman. Leonard Hill, London, 1961.
*Manuscripts* (volumes of notes, drawings, cuttings etc.). P. W. Reynolds. Deposited in the Victoria & Albert Museum, London.
*Military Drawings and Paintings in the Royal Collection.* A. E. H. Miller and N. P. Dawnay. Phaidon Press, London, 1966.
*The Uniforms and History of the Scottish Regiments.* R. M. Barnes and C. K. Allen. Seeley Service, London, 1956.

There have also been published numerous series of military prints and drawings, among which are:
*Cavalry Uniforms of the British Army* by P. G. Smitherman, Hugh Evelyn, London.
*Infantry Uniforms of the British Army* by P. H. Smitherman. (3 series: 1660–1790; 1790–1850; 1850–1960) Hugh Evelyn, London.
*Colored plates of American uniforms, with historical notes* by H. C. McBarron. American Army publication, 1967.
*North's 'Paint-Your-Own' Uniform Cards* and *Military Uniform Charts* by René North, London.
The Hugh Evelyn prints have been published in book form.

# INDEX

Page numbers in bold type refer to illustrations.

Activa Regiment 54
Aiguilettes 93, 154
Albert, Prince 58
Algeria 59
Algeria, Conquest of 52–53
Allen, Ethan 26
Alpins 134
American Revolution 22–27
Arm of Service 154
Artillery matross 4
Austrian Knot 107, 154
Austrian Succession, War of the 12

Baden infantry 97
Balaclava 65
Balkan Wars 122–129
Bandsmen 48, 49
Bavarian infantry 95, 146
Bearskin 32, 154
Bell-topped Shako 154
Bengal 73
Berdan's Sharpshooters 86
Bersaglieri 120, 120, 121, 145
Blenheim 8
'Blue Devils' 134
Board of Ordnance 4, 24
Boer War 102–105
Boers 104
Bombay Sappers and Miners 109, 110
Bosnia 130
Bosnian infantry 151
Boxer Rebellion 108–115
Brabant Rebellion 28
Brandenburg Infantry 146
Browne, Sam 73
Busby 35, 47, 61, 93, 154

Caçadores 45
Californian Lancers 54
Cameron Highlanders 86
Cantinière 75, 75, 154
Cap-Lines 154
Carabiniers 38
Cavalry 19, 23
Cazadores 101
Champagne, Régiment de 10
Charles VI 12
Charles XII 6
Chasseurs 34, 39, 53, 60, 134, 154
Chechia 60, 154
Chevaulegers 97, 147
Civil War, American 82–89
Cockade 154
Comb 154
Concord 22
Confederate Army 84–88

Cossacks 42–43, 64
Crest 154
Crimean War 58
Crow's Foot 154
Cuffs 106–107
Cuff-Slash 154
Cuirassiers 35, 38, 40
Czapka 36, 154

Danish Duchies, War of 78
De Meuron's Regiment 57
Diesbach, Régiment de 20
Dolman 154
Dragoons 7, 12, 16, 19, 23, 25, 33, 38, 59
Drums 65

East-Asian Brigade 112, 112
Epaulettes 61, 65, 92, 93, 106–107, 154
Evzones 122, 123

Facings 155
Fez 121, 129, 151
Field Officer 155
Finsbury Rifles 132
Flank Companies 155
Foreign Legion 53, 111, 112
Franco-Austrian War 74
Franco-German War 90
Frederick the Great 18, 19, 20, 21
French and Indian War 14
Fusiliers 4, 18, 20

Gallipoli 133, 152
Garde du Corps 139
Garde Mobile 90, 92
Gardeschütze-Bataillon 57
Gorget 155
Great Northern War 6
Green Mountain Boys 26, 26
Grenadiers 6, 15, 17, 18, 41
Guadalajara Regiment 54
Guards 10, 33, 59
Gurkhas 71, 72

Hackle 155
Headdresses 66
Helmets 66
Hessian Regiment 25
Highland Light Infantry 103
Highlanders 31
Hodson's Horse 68, 69
Hussars 19, 20, 35, 41, 59

Imperial Guard (France) 75
Indian Mutiny 68
Indian troops 109
Indians, American 15
Infantérie Coloniale 111
Infernales 51
Inniskilling Dragoons 59, 102

International Red Cross 77
Italo-Turkish War 120–121
Italy 62, 74

Jäger 76, 81, 139
Joseph II 29

Kepi 66, 84, 155
Khaki 70
King's African Rifles 133
King's Royal Rifle Corps 14
Kukri 72
Kurta 71
Kut-el-Amara 152

Lace, Regimental 155
Lancers 34, 39, 41, 59
Latin America 50–51
Lexington 22
Light Brigade 58
Lithuanian Regiment 117
Loops 106–107, 155
Louis XV 12
Louisiana Tigers 89

Marines 14
Marlborough, Duke of 8
Massachusetts Iron Brigade 86
Matross 4, 5, 155
Mexican War 54
Minden 20
Mirliton 34, 155
Mississippi Rifles 89
Musketeers 18

Napoleon I 30, 36
Napoleon III 74, 90, 97
Napoleonic Wars 30
Narva, the 6
Neuchâtel 57
New Brunswich Scottish 133
New York Regiment 26
Nigeria Regiment 133

Orange Free State 104
Orléans, Chasseurs d' 53
Orleans Dragoons 17
Overalls 155

Pagri 155
Pavia Hussars 101
Pelisse 155
Peter the Great 7
Picardie Regiment 10
Pickelhaube 19, 73, 80, 94, 147, 155
Piedmont Regiment 5
Piffers 72
Pith helmet 103
Plastron 155
Poltava 6
Pomeranian Regiment 44
Poshteen 155

Princesa Hussars **101**
Punjab Irregular Force 72
Puttees 137

Quebec 16

Rhode Island Artillery **26**
Rifle 155
Rifle Brigade **103**
Roger's Rangers 15, **15**
Rough Riders 99
Roy, Régiment du **12**
Royal American Regiment 14
Royal Artillery **23**, 24, 33
Royal Canadian Mounted Police 142
Royal Horse Artillery **39**
Royal Marine Artillery **108**
Royal Roussillon Regiment **16**, 17
Royal Scots Greys 132
Royal Sussex Regiment 16
Russo-Japanese War 116

Sarre, Régiment de la 17
Saxe, Maurice de 12
Saxon infantry **95**
Schwerin, Regiment von **19**
Scots Greys 59
Sepoys **60**, **109**, 155
Seven Years War 18
Shako 32, 33, 41, 61, 136, 141, 155
Shoulder Straps **106–107**, 155
Silesian Regiment **44**
South African War 102–105
Spahis 93
Spanish Succession, War of the 8
Spanish-American War 98–101
Sumter, Fort 83
Swallows'-Nests 155
Sword-Knot 155

Swords **40**

Taylor, Zachary 55
Tennessee Artillery **85**
Ticonderoga, Fort 22, 26
Tirailleur **91**, 92
Tongerloo Dragoon **28**, 29
Touraine Regiment **20**
Transvaal 104, **105**
Trews 104
Tricorne **66**
Turban 155
Turnbacks 155

Uhlans 80, 147
Ulanka 80
Uniform clothing 4
Uniforms, Argentina **51**
Uniforms, Austria **11**, **12**, 38–39, 40–41, 56, **67**, **77** 79–80, **132**, 133
Uniforms, Austria-Hungary 150–151
Uniforms, Belgium 29, 45–46, 140–141
Uniforms, Britain **9**, 13, 19 30, 48, 58–59, **67**, 68–69, 103–105, **106–107**, 130–131
Uniforms, Bulgaria 126–127, **152**, 153
Uniforms, China 115
Uniforms, Denmark 81
Uniforms, France **10**, **12**, 34–37, 52–53, **60**, **67**, 74–75, 90–93, **106–107**, 110, 134–137
Uniforms, Germany **106–107**, **111**, **112**, 146–149
Uniforms, Greece 122–123
Uniforms, Hungary 19, **67** 76
Uniforms, Italy 113, **114**, **120**, 144, **145**
Uniforms, Japan 113–115, **118–119**, 145, **145**

Uniforms, Mexico **50**, 54–55
Uniforms, Montenegro **129**
Uniforms, Netherlands 45
Uniforms, Norway **67**
Uniforms, Poland 40, 45–46
Uniforms, Portugal 45–46, **144**, 145
Uniforms, Prussia 19, 43–44 57, **67**, 78–80, 94–97
Uniforms, Russia **7**, 41–43, 64–65, **67**, 116–118, 138–139
Uniforms, Sardinia 62–63
Uniforms, Serbia 124–125, **144**
Uniforms, Spain **46**, 47 100–101
Uniforms, Sweden **6**
Uniforms, Switzerland **67**
Uniforms, Turkey 62–63, **121**, **128**, 152, **153**
Uniforms, United States 26, 48–49, 55, 82–89, 98–99, 112–113, 142–143

Van der Noot, Henry 29
Vincent's and Latour's 13
Virginia cavalry **88**
Virginia Regiment **85**

Walloons 11
War of 1812 48
Warner, Seth 26
Washington, George 23
Waterloo 45
Wings **106–107**, 155
Wolfe, James 16
World War I 130–153
Württemberg Guard Artillery **44**

Ypres Volunteers **28**, 29

Zouaves 53, 59–61, **82**, 84 86, 92

# OTHER TITLES IN THE SERIES

The GROSSET ALL-COLOR GUIDES provide a library of authoritative information for readers of all ages. Each comprehensive text with its specially designed illustrations yields a unique insight into a particular area of man's interests and culture.

## NOW AVAILABLE

Prehistoric Animals
Bird Behavior
Wild Cats
Fossil Man
Porcelain
Military Uniforms, 1686–1918
Birds of Prey
Flower Arranging
Microscopes & Microscopic
  Life
The Plant Kingdom
Rockets & Missiles
Flags of the World
Atomic Energy
Weather & Weather
  Forecasting
Trains
Sailing Ships & Sailing
  Craft
Electronics
Myths & Legends of
  Ancient Greece
Cats
Discovery of Africa
Horses & Ponies
Fishes of the World
Astronomy
Snakes of the World
Dogs

## SOON TO BE PUBLISHED

Guns
Exploring the Planets
Discovery of The American
  West
Animals of Australia & New
  Zealand
Jewelry
Warships
Mammals of the World
Trees of the World
Computers at Work
Architecture
Monkeys & Apes
The Animal Kingdom
Discovery of North America
English Victoriana
Natural History Collecting
Myths & Legends of
  Ancient Egypt
The Human Body
Tropical Aquarium Fishes
African Animals
Polar Animals
Myths & Legends of the
  South Seas
Myths & Legends of Rome
Myths & Legends of India
Arms & Armor
Discovery of South America